Byzantium

Byzantium

Text by **Pierre/Janine Soisson**

Translated by David Macrae

Minerva

Contents

Credits : Alinari 51a, 123, 124, 128, 131b, 132, 144 - Anderson 6, 61, 78a, b, c, 84, 88, 97, 114, 130, 131a - Archives 29, 44, 48, 50, 67, 77 - Fiore 62, 68, 69, 81, 109, 127 - Harlingue 58 - Roger-Viollet 2, 5, 7, 10a, b, 14, 18, 21, 22, 23, 24, 25, 26, 30a, b, 32, 54, 94, 100, 102, 104, 107, 108, 110, 113, 118, 119, 120, 125, 129, 134, 136, end papers - S.E.F. 35, 47, 51b, 53, 91, 139 - Spectra 72, 74, 92 - Unedi 13, 17, 27, 36, 55, 70, 71, 73, 80, 98, 126.

Printer, industria gráfica, sa
Tuset, 19 Barcelona Sant Vicenç dels Horts 1976
Depósito legal B. 49843-1976
Printed in Spain

Introduction

The name Byzantium conjures up images of gilded cupolas casting reflections of the setting sun in the waters of the Sea of Marmara; it brings to mind memories of a refined, decadent civilization, dominated by the lavish splendor of Theodora, with her ornate, jewel-studded elegance, and by the most pointless discussions about the sex of angels.

The history of the Byzantine Empire is not very familiar to the general public. What seems now to have been a fleeting, unreal moment actually lasted for more than a thousand years. It is the longest period of the history of the world's most prestigious empire: Rome.

This was the Rome which turned a barbarous continent into the Western World.

Why did Constantine decide to transfer his capital from the banks of the Tiber to the shores of the Bosphorus?

Why was it that this great Roman Empire, founded by the mighty legions, consolidated by Roman law and the *Pax Romana,* and developed by the toil of its peasant-soldiers, fell apart, shrank and then shrivelled up to nothing?

How did the Cross come to replace the She-Wolf, and an age of warriors give way to an age of monks?

How did *homo christianicus* succeed

Byzantine decorative motif (Church of St. Lephteris, Athens).

in supplanting *homo romanus?*

Why was it that, one day in 1453, the remains of the greatest empire in history, now reduced to a single walled city, at last feel before the onslaught of the Turks and Islam?

The reader should not expect to find in this brief volume an exhaustive history of Byzantium: tome upon tome would be required to give a full account of this empire, together with its causes and its consequences.

Here we have simply tried to sketch out the main features of a period in history which is still inadequately known—the history of a civilisation which has left a distinct mark on every single member of Western society. We have merely tried to raise the corner of the veil surrounding the rise and fall of Byzantium the Golden.

Early Bizantine decoration (Rome).

1/One empire succeeds another

The Byzantine Empire succeeded the Empire of Rome; yet, even though the reign of Constantine marked the foundation of a new capital and the coming of a new civilisation, there was no clear split between the two empires. It was to take three centuries for the heritage of Rome, now under barbarian attack, to be passed on to Byzantium.

This process began after the reign of the Antonines, at a time when the Pax Romana was at its height, late in the 2nd century. The Empire was about to pass through a number of terrible crises: Emperors came and went, at the whim of the Pretorians and the soldiers who made and un-made them as they pleased. This was because, ever since its foundation by Augustus, the Empire had suffered from a grave flaw: the lack of a rule governing the succession.

This instability of political authority led to heightened pressure from the barbarians, who mangled the *limes* drawn up by Hadrian. Italy and even Rome itself were threatened. Orderly economic life was brought to a halt, taxes were no longer collected and the countryside was abandoned. As for spiritual matters, the old civil religion—which had formed a traditional and mystical link among the citizens—also collapsed. In a quest for other-worldly consolation for the distress of

Statue of Roman emperor outside the Istanbul Museum.

View of the Bosphorus from Istanbul.

the moment, men's minds turned to oriental superstitions, moving away from naturalistic pantheism. Gradually, the Christian religion infiltrated all levels of society.

It is true that Diocletian made a bold, and to some extent successful attempt to introduce reforms, in order to stop the decadence of the Empire. He fought against anarchy and strove to present to the people a new image of the Emperor—a semi-divine person, venerated like an oriental potentate before whom all men prostrate themselves. During his reign, the Emperor ceased to respect the forms of the Republic, which is something that even his proudest predecessors had always done. He gave the Empire a truly monarchical constitution, thus eventually causing the advent of an administration which was so highly centralized that it became impossible to entrust to a single man the awesome task of governing such a vast expanse of territory.

For this reason, in 293, Diocletian took a step which foreshadowed the Byzantine Empire: he appointed Maximian as his right-hand man. Like the Emperor, Maximian bore the name Augustus; he was given authority over the territory of the northern Mediterranean, while Diocletian remained in charge of the south. Here we have the beginnings of a split; moreover, significantly enough, the Greek East began to achieve predominance over the Latin West.

Thenceforth, the changing fortunes of the Roman Empire were in the hands of two men named Augustus, each of whom was assisted by a *Caesar* who could, if necessary, replace them. Here we have the seeds of the schism between the two parts of this colossal State.

This is why Constantine, the successor of Diocletian, had a number of very good reasons, as we shall see, for leaving Rome and moving his capital, his political and administrative center and his place of residence to Byzantium.

After a while, he forgot that he was the Augustus of only the East and that another Augustus, Licinius, shared the Empire with him. Both men actually had only one thought in their minds, that of seizing power over the whole of the Empire. Civil war therefore became inevitable: it broke out in 324. After successive defeats at Andrinople and Chrysopolis, Licinius eventually surrendered to Constantine, who, conveniently forgetting his commitments, had him executed, and, some time later, his son Licinius the Younger, in order to be doubly sure.

Constantine was now sole Emperor.

Two views of the Bosphorus near the Black Sea.

He had already appointed his third son, Constance, as Caesar. He was entirely free to alter the old Roman Empire as he pleased; and he soon set about this task with relish.

For a few decades Constantine and his mother Helen were ranked as saints of the Christian religion. According to certain interested sources, during the battle at Milvius bridge, against Maxentius, Constantine is supposed to have seen a luminous cross in the sky, with these words written above it in letters of fire:

"By this sign you shall conquer".

At this point he is said to have ordered his soldiers to reproduce this sign on their shields, while he himself became converted as soon as victory was assured, giving the impression that he was making an act of submission to a new god.

However, it is much more likely that the only vision Constantine ever had took place in a Gaulish sanctuary at Trèves in 310, during which Apollo appeared to the febrile imagination of the future emperor; the god was holding in his hand a laurel crown, which Constantine regarded as symbolic of supreme power.

When he later became the sole master of the Empire, he was an unabashed devotee of paganism, with particular emphasis on sun worship. Coins from this period show an effigy of the Emperor linked to that of Apollo.

The Christian historian Lactantius reports Constantine's vision as a mere dream as a result of which he was inspired to have the shields of his troops marked with "the letter X crossed at the top with a curving stroke–a sign which was soon to become the monogram of Constantine. The reader who so desires can see in it the first two letters of the name Christ, in Greek.

Christian tradition is wrong to claim that the faith of Christ was first given official tolerance during the reign of Constantine. It was actually Galerius who, having inflicted severe ill-treatment on the Christians through the edicts of 303 and 304, then issued the first edict of tolerance, in April 311. Henceforth, Christians were allowed to hold meetings, provided that they did not disturb the public order and included the Emperor in their prayers to their god. How can one account for this sudden change on the part of Galerius? One possible explanation is the serious and painful illness which had greatly weakened him and was shortly to lead to his death. Apart from which, the people were tired of the persecutions which were now manifestly pointless.

A bust of Emperor Constantine.

Another point on which Christian tradition is in error is the claim that the Edict of Milan (313) constituted formal proof of Constantine's conversion... The text of this Edict, which has been preserved for us by Lactantius and Eusebius, accords no special privileges to the Christian form of worship, but merely proclaims freedom of conscience in matters of religion and orders the return of property confiscated from Christians. Moreover, this document was not the work of Constantine but of Licinius and dates from the time of his struggle against Maximinus Gaia. We know that, in the year 313, negotiations were held in Milan between Constantine and Licinius; we also have, from that same year, a prayer, the text of which was handed down to us by Lactantius and which is thought to have been composed by Licinius on the eve of his battle with Maximinus Gaia. Yet the prayer makes not the slightest reference to the Christian religion, and is merely an invocation of some supreme god who could well be any one of a number of gods, such as Mithra, Jupiter, Javeh or Jesus. Even so, this text does show the emergence of a new type of religious thinking.

There can be no doubt that Constantine was familiar with these two texts and indeed approved them, but this does not amount to evidence of his conversion. In addition, we also have a piece of gold jewelry made in the imperial goldsmith's shop at Tarragona, also dated 313, which shows Constantine twinned with Apollo.

It was only after 320 that Constantine began to veer towards Christianity, though, even after his victory over Licinius in 324, he did not impose the new religion. He did, on the other hand, guarantee the right to practice the religion of one's choice. Moreover, throughout his entire reign, he remained the "Pontifex Maximus", or supreme pontiff of the classic Roman religion, and he himself exercised the rituals for the worship of Jupiter Capitolinus.

The fact is that Constantine, who was always a sympathizer, received baptism from an Arian bishop only on the day before his death. Under his rule, however, the Christian community benefitted from the liberal attitudes of the governmental authorities and succeeded in growing, erecting great numbers of churches. It seems certain that this growth was fairly disorderly, with a flood of different sects and countless heresies. This was the origin of the Byzantinism which we shall refer to later.

Constantine therefore did not make Christianity a State religion at any

time during his reign. Even so, while taking care to keep the favor of the supporters of the old forms of worship, of which he was the Pontifex Maximus, he arranged for the State to be able to supervise and check into the new religious organisation, thereby imposing interference by the temporal authorities in the affairs of the Church. This was a most ingenious policy; however, it had a corollary, in that it meant Christian opinion would be able to exercise certain influence. This was to cause him many a headache later on.

After the Council of Nicaea, Constantine forbade the gladiatorial games. This was an unpopular decree, because

Early reconstitution of Constantinople.

the common people adored the circus games. He also made it unlawful for officers and generals to demands foodstuffs and money from the populace.

Family discord also entered into the picture. Constantine's second wife, Fausta, accused Crispus, her husband's eldest son, of attempting to seduce her, whereupon Constantine had the offending young man put to death—rashly, as it turned out, because it soon became apparant that the empress had been lying all along. So she also was put to death.

This was a mistake which pleased no-one, and gave people the impression that Constantine was a nasty, hotheaded sovereign. The Romans seized this pretext eagerly in order to vent their anger on an emperor who was opposed to their games. Constantine was insulted and booed in the streets of Rome—a state of affairs which he found difficult to tolerate. However, despite the advice of his closest relatives, he did not order reprisals.

Yet he did decide to break with the cradle and the center of the Empire, and vowed to leave Rome. When he eventually did so, he was never to return.

In 328, in Byzantium, he laid the foundations of a new capital, which was to bear his name: Constantinople.

2/Constantinople

Byzantium was a former colony of Megara and was founded in 660 BC by Byzas. It was successively a Persian, Lacedemonian, Athenian and Roman colony. Severus laid siege to it and virtually destroyed it, though, later on, he did a great deal of construction there.

The city had barely been rebuilt when Gallienus wrecked its walls again. The Heruleans sacked it; then Licinius made it his headquarters. Constantine was not, therefore, about to build an entirely new city, but his projected expansions and transformations were so sweeping that one can truly talk about the construction of a new city.

The actual work of building—commensurate with the Emperor's plans—lasted thirty years.

First, he greatly enlarged the area within the city limits. To those who wondered at these unbelievable dimensions he would reply, according to Christian tradition: "I shall go on until the invisible God, who walks before me, feels the moment has come to stop me."

Whether or not he was acting out of obedience to this god or that, he covered the city with prestigious buildings and structures. At a single stroke, he recruited 40,000 Goths for earth-moving operations. It was clear that he intended to eclipse the brilliance of Rome. He himself drew the outline of the new city, the total area of which was to be five times greater than that of the old city. Like Rome, Constantinople was to have seven hills and fourteen regions, and also a Capitol. Two sumptuous buildings were set aside specially for the Senate, looking onto a vast public square surrounded by columns and statues which had been brought there from all the corners of the Empire–as Constantine saw nothing wrong in such looting: this was the Augusteon. The statue of Princess Helen, the Emperor's mother, stood at the top of a column of porphyry, opposite the statue of her son.

In the center of the city another square, this time circular in shape– the Hall of Constantine– had a statue of the Emperor in the middle. As an interesting aside, it should be noted that this statue had originally been of Apollo of Illium; all that happened was that the head was changed and a piece of the true cross was sealed in its base–a curious merger of religions! This relic also has its own history. Under the consulate of Maxentius and Maxim, Princess Helen, on a trip to Palestine, was astounded to see that the pagans had built a temple to Venus on Mount Golgotha, the place near Jerusalem where Christ had been

Byzantine couple, VI century: styles of dress were already the same as this at the end of the Roman Empire.

ΕΥΡΕϹΙϹ

crucified. According to Christian tradition, the indignant princess had the temple razed to the ground and the statues it contained destroyed. Excavations led to the discovery of the sepulcher in which Joseph of Arimathea had Christ buried, together with his cross and those of the two thieves. This is the origin of the relic which was inserted at the base of the statue of Constantine.

Christian tradition also maintained that Constantine had the nails found on the cross attached to his helmet. Empress Helen was an exceedingly high-powered discoverer of relics, as those which she is supposed to have found include not just the crown of thorns but even the basket which Christ used for the multiplication of the loaves and the fishes. As we shall see, Constantinople was an avid consumer of sacred objects.

However, let us revert to the new city, with its dazzling brilliance. A very broad avenue, the Mese (middle way) went from the Augusteon to the four public squares. Against a background of the porticoes and terraces of the superb residences of the Senators, it ran from the Golden Miliary, the monument which showed the distances from the capital to the main cities of the Empire.

The Emperor's Palace stood at the

Remains of the Byzantine walls of Istanbul.

Inside the Cathedral of Hagia Sophia.

water's edge, and a person standing on one of its terraces could see both Europe and Asia at the same time. It is rather a medley of styles spread out over 1 1/2 square miles, on the mesa overlooking the Bosphorus. It had eight inner courtyards and a number of rooms intended for a range of purposes... including six prisons!

The grand main entrance opened onto the Augusteon through a huge bronze gate, the Chalaea. Everywhere one turned there was marble, porphyry, mosaics and colonnades. However, the prize item of the palace was the throne room, which was adorned with unbelievable splendor. The throne itself stood on a dais six steps high, sheltered in an alcove and surrounded by palmtrees, lions and griffons made of gold. On major state occasions, these objects were articulated by means of an ingenious mechanism. Another system raised the royal throne and lowered the crown until it was just level with the monarch's forehead. The crowd was obviously duly impressed by what they saw. On special ceremonial days the royal treasures were displayed in large glass cases behind the Emperor. In the middle of the room there was a huge gem-encrusted cross attached to the cupola. The entire room was adorned with statues of Pythian Apollo, the Muses of Hellicon, the Delphi Tripod, all taken from the temples in which they had originally been situated.

Nothing remains of this palace today: it has suffered the same fate as the Empire itself. During the decline of the Empire, the last emperors neglected these superb buildings, and even stooped to selling off their treasures and chopping up priceless furniture for firewood! All we can do is dream of what it must have been like.

Of all the churches of the city, the most famous and the biggest was Hagia Sophia. This "wonder of the world" is a unique monument, of rare artistic beauty. It was built by Constance, son of Constantine, but was twice destroyed by fire, during rebellions, in 404 and 532. Justinian the Great rebuilt it on a larger scale, with even greater magnificence. In so doing, he requisitioned all land and structures near the building and brought along ten thousand workers who were under the orders of the Syrian architect Anthemius.

Work lasted five years, ten months and ten days, and consumed 452 quintals of gold. There can be no doubt that the taxpayers of the entire Empire bore a heavy burden about this time!

An oval courtyard surrounded with porticoes leads to a central nave 75 yards square, crowned with a cupola

محمد
الله

Left: inside Cathedral of Hagia Sophia, the "Columns of Ephesus". Right: the Istanbul Aqueduct.

100 feet in diameter, a masterpiece of equilibrium. There are balconies around the nave at lower levels.

Hagia Sophia was originally decorated with incredible riches, including sumptuous amounts of marble, gold plate, precious stones, enamels, silk and gold cloth. However, its most spectacular feature was its illumination by night: according to Procopius, a whole array of chandeliers glittered "with dazzling splendor".

With the passage of time the building was to suffer martyrdom on several occasions; after the fires which devastated the original structure, it was to be severely damaged by the Iconoclasts. The Crusaders, for their part, acted like brazen plunderers. This church, which had been profaned by the Western Christians, was to be the scene of horrible acts or revenge. Attempts are now being made to restore it, and it has recently been given the status of a museum.

In keeping with the Roman model, a general sewage system was installed, discharging into the sea. Water was distributed by a large number of aqueducts. There were also numerous public baths. But the place most preferred by the common people, their true palace, was the Hippodrome. Here they truly felt they were in their element. A great number of public

events were held at the Hippodrome.

This structure was the work of Septimus Severus, 120 years before Constantine, and was an imitation of the Circus Maximus in Rome. The circus was nearly 600 yards long and the arena itself measured about 480 yards by 90. It was ringed by some 40 rows of marble seats, and the entire structure was dominated by a tower which stood over the main entrance. At the top of this tower stood the famous bronze quadriga, the history of which is so well known. It was originally removed from the island of Chios by Theodosius I, and later taken by the Venetians to their own island in 1204. Napoleon transported it to Paris, but it was returned to Venice in 1814.

Stables attached to the Hippodrome were used only on the day before the races. A large promenade ran all of the way around the Hippodrome. On the left was the imperial box, which was directly linked to the palace.

Here again, it was the Crusaders who took it upon themselves to loot

The burnt column of Constantine at Istanbul and one of the walls of the Castle of the Seven Towers.

and destroy the greatest circus in the world.

In order to encourage people to settle in the new city Constantine seized eagerly upon any idea which was likely to achieve this purpose. The territory of the town was considered to be Italic, and was therefore exempt from taxes. By means of a highly arbitrary decree, the emperor denied all property-owners in Asia who did not own a house in Constantinople the right to make a will. Other similar decrees guaranteed the success of the new city. Rome lost none of its privileges, but Constantinople enjoyed exactly the same kind as the older city. Official propaganda was in operation full-time.

In order to pay for the prodigious expenses involved in this "renewal", the whole Empire was heavily taxed. No-one, however poor, escaped this burden—including the beggars. Only Constantinople was exempt from this tribute: since its inhabitants were not required to pay any taxes at all, whether direct or indirect, they were in effect the only ones who did not pay for the luxury which they were about to enjoy.

We should not exaggerate the "anti-Roman" feelings of Constantine when attempting to account for his decision to remove from Rome its title of

capital. It is also wrong to attribute it to the Emperor's desire to build a Christian capital—the version of his thinking found in Christian tradition. Constantine was really moved by strategic, economic and political considerations.

The Goths and the Persians were a constant threat to the Empire, and Rome was too far away to serve as a base for its defense. Moreover, Rome was directly exposed to attack from the Germanic hordes, whereas Constantinople, which was well protected against invasions, was a superb strategic site from which expeditions could be sent against enemies in the north and the east.

Apart from this, Constantinople controlled the straits and thus guaranteed freedom of trade between Europe and Asia, the Mediterranean and the Black Sea.

Lastly, when compared to the declining, ancient civilisation in which Rome was situated, the Orient, with its wealth and culture, seemed to hold a much more promising future.

It was not until 395 that the Byzantine Empire officially came into being, when the Roman Empire was divided into two separate States. Its importance grew *pari passu* with the collapse of the Western Empire. This heightened influence can be placed fairly accurately in the year 476, when Odoacer sent Zeno, the Eastern Emperor, the imperial insignia.

But Constantinople's noble lineage can be traced back before that time. L. Bréhier writes that: "On the coins of the year 330 there are two cities, in the form of busts bearing laurels wreaths and helmets, and covered with the imperial mantle. But Constantinople is the one carrying the scepter."

3/The Basileus and his House

While it is true that the new civilisation of which Constantinople was the cradle was undoubtedly Eastern, Hellenistic and Christian, it did, nonetheless, draw heavily on the remaining vitality of the Latin world. From its early years it was to attract the wealth, prestige and the entire heritage of the ancient world. This new empire, which was highly organised and firmly based on an implacable pyramidal hierarchy, was to last for eleven centuries and withstand the numerous and repeated attacks of the Visigoths, Burgondes, Suebi, Vandals, Ostrogoths and Avars. Its enemies included the Genovese, the Lombards and the Venetians; it finally succumbed only to the massive onslaught of Arabs, Persians and Turks. Moreover, this list of its foes is not exhaustive: the new empire must, therefore, have been solidly built.

At the pinnacle of power stood the Emperor, with all manner of magnificence and pomp. He took the name of Basileus, from a Greek word meaning "king" when Heraclius I had defeated the Persians in 630. He was the elected one of Providence, the living Law, and absolute Authority. This had the effect of making any usurper who succeeded in grabbing power for himself totally legitimate and beyond all challenge—once he had succeeded, that is. Such occurrences

Remains of the Palace of Constantine at Istanbul. Right: one of the first of the Byzantine emperors.

Scene in the imperial palace: conspirators being watched by spies.

were frequent and, for safety's sake, were accompanied by the rapid removal from the scene of the usurper's predecessor. The new occupant of the imperial throne had absolute powers, in that he could associate anyone he chose with the throne, and he could also delegate authority as he saw fit. Michael the Drunk, for example, decided that his companion in debauchery, Basil, would be associated with the throne; on Michael's orders, Basil had married the emperor's former mistress, Ingerine. The irony here lies in the fact that Basil grew to be passionately fond of the exercise of authority, changed beyond recognition and became an excellent emperor. In so doing, he was obliged to rid himself of his former master—by the dagger—and to order the execution of a new favorite, Basilician, another inveterate drinker.

When circumstances were favorable, the emperor sought to create an imperial line of descent; however, if no child was born, or if the only such child was not yet old enough to reign, or if he whished to disinherit an eligible child, he could choose his own successor.

The emperor was virtually divine, and his authority reached even into the Church. Everything pertaining to him was sacred: his residence was the Sacred Palace, the minister of finance was known as the Count of Sacred Generosity, the grand chamberlain was the Count of the Sacred Chamber. Just as the treasury of the State and the emperor's own fortune were merged together, so also the administrative center and the imperial residence were both housed in the same building. This was where the Basileus held his political councils, administered justice and conducted his affairs.

The Imperial Palace—the Court—became the center of the State; in the words of Victor Duruy, "the entire Empire fitted into it". All officials were linked to the palace and held a rank at court, and a title of nobility attached to his official denomination: instead of serving the Empire, he served the Emperor. The former "clients" of the Roman sovereigns were now the "companions" of the Basileus. The word "count" derives from this notion.

The companions were organised in a precise hierarchy, based solely on official position. In the immediate entourage of the Emperor were the members of his family, the Nobilissimes. They were followed by the Patricians, the Illustres, the Respectabiles, the Clarissimes and the Perfectissimes.

The distrustful Basileus never officially appointed a prime minister as such, but, depending on circumstan-

ces and on his pleasure, he did entrust the cares of government to a palace official.

Besides this crowd of notables there was the vast flock of pages, ushers and servants of all sorts, and also the eunuchs, who, according to Libanius, were more numerous than the flies in summer.

The count of the domestic infantry and the count of the domestic cavalry each had 3,500 men under their command—usually Armenians—who paraded magnificently outside the palace gates. This system of government by the members of the imperial household is a typically oriental and Hellenistic institution.

The régime was actually less rigorous than might have seemed the case, as it was attenuated by endless traditions. For example, the Basileus himself limited his own authority by granting numerous privileges to the top-ranking ecclesiastics.

He also allowed popular rallies which were held in the Hippodrome; they acted as a kind of public opinion poll which kept the prince informed about the popularity of the various reforms which he sought to introduce. At such gatherings his people freely expressed their opinions, dividing into two factions, the Blues and the Greens, depending on the color of the jacket

Byzantine copper coin from the 8th century, bearing an effigy of Leo, Emperor of Byzantium.

worn by the chariot drivers. On the whole, the common people, the opposition and the revolutionaries were green while the aristocracy was blue, though the divisions could vary.

During a famous episode in Byzantine history, under Justinian in January 532, the people, groaning under the burden of taxation, was most decidedly green. They detested the imperial ministers, in particular a certain John of Cappadocia, a favorite of Justinian, who was accused, probably with good reason, of selling justice. At the circus games, Justinian declared himself in favor of the blues, while Theodora, his wife–the beautiful, glorious Theodora of whom we shall speak later–supported the greens. However, this gesture did not suffice to prevent the crowd from greeting the emperor with murmurings of discontent, to put it mildly. The sovereign sought to restore silence, but was booed down.

The prefect then tried to intimidate the mob by choosing at random three of the demonstrators whom he sent for execution. The crowd, in response to this most unhappy initiative, started rampaging through the streets. Two of the condemned men were freed by force and the doors of the prisons were thrown open. The rioters even went so far as to set fire to the palace. Shouting "Nika" (be victorious) the people repelled the attacks of the Herulean soldiers. The Emperor, who was supposed to wield absolute power, was so overwhelmed by these events that, three days later, he returned to the Hippodrome to promise a complete amnesty. To his dismay he was greeted with a barrage of insults: the people, their trust thoroughly, destroyed, preferred to name another sovereign, Hepatius.

In utter disarray, Justinian, abandoning all notions of the sacred imperial personality, devoted his energies entirely to flight. A boat was waiting for him in the harbor; his ministers and "companions" packed their bags.

That day, Justinian would have lost his throne had it not been for the vigor shown by Theodora, who, quivering with indignation, burst in upon her husband and those who were preparing for an emergency departure and rebuked them: "He who has been invested with sovereign power should not be allowed to survive if it is taken away from him... The imperial purple is the finest of burial-shrouds."

The men were all galvanized by her voice and their courage returned. The famous general Belisarius rounded up his troops and led them to the circus which he then surrounded. The populace, drunk with victory, excitement and wine, was still inside, its thoughts

Early print of Leo III the Isaurian.

more on inspiring speeches than on guarding the stairs leading to the circus. Belisarius moved in swiftly and easily and, from the top of the banked marble seats sent a hail of deadly arrows down on the crowd, killing many of the rioters on the spot. Those that tried to escape were intercepted at the gates and mercilessly cut down. There were more than 30,000 dead.

The list of Byzantine emperors is lengthy and their reigns were for the most part marked by sharp fluctuations of fate. Take for example Constantine VII. On the death of his father, Leo VI the Wise, in 912, he was only six, so his uncle Alexander became his tutor and reigned in his place. Under his leadership, however, the court simply went to pieces, as he placed immense trust in charlatans and astrologers, and, worse still, he conferred power on seven favorites. Luckily, he died in 913. The young emperor did not seem to mind the state of affairs bequeathed to him by his regent, but he did call for his mother Zoe, widow of Leo, who had been exiled. The tutelary council agreed to send for her. As soon as she arrived at the palace, this energetic woman took complete charge of affairs, by expelling the tutors and seizing power for herself. Her conduct of the war against the Bulgars and the Muslims was truly outstanding; indeed, she was often in the front line of battle with her troops.

She might perhaps have waited for her son to come of age and then hand the throne back to him, had it not been for her meeting with a handsome young naval commander, Romanus Lecapenus. It appears that he had just been heavily defeated by the Bulgars, and stood accused of treason. The Senate sentenced him to have his eyes gouged out, whereupon Zoe first caught sight of him, fell in love with him, saved him from his terrible fate and even gave him a fleet which, this time, he led to victory. Thereafter she could refuse no favor to the handsome general. His influence was so great that he arranged for his daughter Helen to marry the young prince, thus acquiring for him the distinguished title of "Father of the Emperor".

Having consolidated his position he jettisoned the aging Zoe whose love he now found overbearing. On his orders, she was shaved bald and shut up in a cloister. Romanus, who had become the absolute master of the child-king, obtained from him the title of Caesar and became associated with the Empire in 920. Thenceforth, Romanus Lecapenus governed alone. He did balk at associating two of his sons, Stephen and Constantine, with the Empire (944), while appointing the

third, who was a mere adolescent, Patriarch of Constantinople. This young man, finding the sacred rites boring, decided to introduce into them a number of dances, popular songs and assorted choirs. Sometimes he would interrupt the mass in order to go and visit his stables, where he was reputed to have kept two thousand horses.

Meanwhile, houng Constantine VII was left to his studies, and drew such a low allowance that he had to sell his own paintings in order to survive.

He eventually tired of the Bohemian life, and, in 944, he formed an alliance with Stephen, one of Romanus' sons who aspired to overthrow their father. The conspiracy succeeded. Romanus suddenly found himself in a monastery on the island of Pelea, while Constantine was on the throne. He continued his association with the two sons of the now banished Romanus, showing no rancor. However, the two sons began to plot against him, so that the Emperor eventually had them sent away and flogged. He then reigned alone, though he was always very much under the influence of his wife, Helen Lecapenus, since he himself was quite a weak character.

Anecdotes such as these make it clear that the exercise of absolute royalty in Byzantium was no holiday. In most cases, each newcomer to the

Emperor Justinian on his throne surrounded by his court (miniature from the manuscript Justinianus Institutiones. *Left: detail from this miniature.*

Detail from a mosaic in the great apse of Hagia Sophia, depicting Empress Irene.

imperial throne, whether a usurper or an appointee, swiftly moved to rid himself of his rival, who was sent off into exile, usually having had his eyes gouged out first. Sometimes his nose was chopped off. The story of Justinian II, however, shows that such misfortunes did not always suffice to deter a prince in his quest for power. This Basileus, who lived the luxurious life of an oriental potentate, one day had the unlikely idea of massacring the entire population of Constantinople which, groaning under the burden of taxes, had risen in revolt. Ruscius, the commander of his guard, refused to carry out this order. The city rebelled and Justinian was led in chains to the Hippodrome. Out of respect for the memory of his father, Constantine IV, who was venerated by the ordinary people, it was decided that his punishment sould be confined merely to the cutting off of his nose—whence his nickname, Rhinotmeta (cut nose). He had reigned for nine years. Yet, later on, he succeeded in returning, with the aid of the king of the Bulgars, Terbel. He raised an army of 15,000 men and entered the Byzantine capital at night, along an unguarded aqueduct, and seized the palace. The crowd, showing remarkable adaptability, acclaimed him as their emperor, with or without his severed nose This second reign, which was to be bathed in the bloodshed of terrible reprisals, did not last long. Justinian II was eventually overthrown and executed, together with his son Tiberius, by his successor Philippicus.

Sometimes castration was used on the high and mighty, but even this form of mutilation was not an absolute deterrent. For example, Michael the Paphlagonian occupied the imperial throne despite the fact that he was a eunuch. He was put on the throne in 1034 by another empress Zoe, whose love for him was, alas, purely platonic.

The commonest procedure and the most effective was the assassination, more or less accompanied by tortures, of the new monarch's predecessor. Nicephorus II was hacked to death by a scimitar in 976, after his bones had been broken with blows from sword-handles, so that General Zimisces could then reign calmly—that is until he in turn was removed from the scene, this time by poisoning. Andronicus I, who had murdered the young emperor Alexius I in 1118, ascended the throne and married the former emperor's wife, Agnes, daughter of Louis VII, king of France. He, in turn, came to a sticky end, when a former favorite of Alexius, Isaac, stirred up a revolt and delivered Andronicus to the crowd, which, displaying both inconstancy and

cruelty, wrenched off his arm, smashed his teeth, cut off his right hand and then hung it from a gibbet before his very eyes. After 48 hours in prison, he had one of his eyes gouged out, and was led out through the streets; he was then dragged by the feet to the circus, where a prostitute poured buckets of scalding water over him, until an officer, moved to compassion, plunged a sword into his heart. Isaac was then crowned emperor.

What is astonishing about these aspirants to the position of Basileus is their courage, or perhaps their total lack of awareness. The chances of dying a natural death were slim indeed for these unfortunates. One readily sympathises with a certain Theodosius, who reigned under the title Theodosius III in 715 and 716. Having been elevated to the throne by some mutinous soldiers who had rebelled against Anastas II, who was in fact quite a competent sovereign, Theodosius turned down the flattering proposal which had been put to him, preferring peace and security to personal glory. Since the soldiers kept insisting, he decided to flee. But the mutinous soldiers went after him and brought him back to Constantinople where, *manu militari,* he was compelled to reign. Still refusing to give in to tradition, he refused to have his predecessor, Anastas, put to death.

Theodosius III was a pious and a good man; yet these were not the

Mosaic from Ravenna showing Theodoric's palace.

qualities sought in a sovereign. Things were going badly for the empire: the war against the Bulgars was being bungled so badly that it was necessary to come to terms with the enemy. The general in charge of the Eastern armies, Leo, refused to recognize Theodosius as his sovereign. He marched on the capital and the Senate begged the emperor to resign in order to avoid the horrors of civil war. Theodosius readily agreed, on condition that his life was spared. In return, it was required of him that he and his children be ordained priests. In this way he lived out his life calmly, copying in golden letters the Gospels and the texts of Holy Office. Leo then reigned for fifteen years, and very successfully, under the famous name of Leo III the Isaurian.

It can be seen that the sacred nature of his office was of little protection to the Basileus. Episodes such as those we have described abounded. Yet, despite the passing of one emperor and the advent of another, the administration had to go on. And it was precisely the administration which provided some guarantee of continuity during the frequent upheavals which afflicted Byzantium. This heritage of the Roman genius was to maintain for many centuries, in the midst of Greek versatility, the mildewed edifice of Empire.

Tax collector in Byzantium.

4/The institutions of Empire the Reforms of Justinian

The Byzantine Empire bore the indelible imprint of the work of Justinian I, or Justinian the Great. This sovereign, who reigned 200 years after the foundation of Constantinople, was to become known to posterity as the one man who did most to give the Eastern Empire its own distinctive internal structure.

Justinian's grand ambition was the reconstitution of the Roman Empire. As he reconquered from the barbarians what had once been the Empire of the Caesars, he set about restoring order and prosperity through the kind of sound management which had been the hallmark of the Pax Romana. His domestic policies were therefore based on two primordial aims: the transformation of the law and administrative reform.

Rome had founded the law, which had given the Empire order and unity. Justinian realized that a lasting State could only be based on a strong legal framework. A century had passed since the publication of the Theodosian Code, and many laws were irrelevant to the new changed circumstances while others had fallen into disuse. Many reforms had been improvised and there was an abundance of contradictory texts. The influence of Christianity had altered the manner in which the thinking of legislators was now interpreted, while Roman law was often severely at variance with the customs of the nations which made up the Empire. The result was a hotchpotch of local and customary legislation which was contrary to the unifying spirit which Justinian had inherited from Latin tradition. This is why, as Bonaparte was to act with French law many centuries later and for the same reasons, the emperor sought to safeguard Roman law, to restore it where it had disappeared and to bring it up to date where necessary.

For this purpose, in 528, one year after his accession to the throne, he appointed ten legal experts whose job it was to systematize, unify, clarify and reform the legislation. The principal jurist involved in this exercise was the questor Tribonian, a curious, highly venal man, virtually an atheist, who, nonetheless, was to be one of the most influential counsellors of Justinian on legislative matters.

The legal achievements of this great reign consist essentially of what later came to be known as the *Corpus Juris Civilis*. It was made up of four parts:

– The *Code of Justinian,* which combined all the imperial constitutions from the time of Hadrian up to 534.

– The *Digest* or *Pandectes,* which represents the sum of all Roman jurisprudence.

Byzantine officials listening to a noble explaining the gospel to them.

– The *Institutions,* which are a treaty of practical law intended for students.

– The *Novella,* or the 154 constitutions published by Justinian himself from 534 onwards.

These latter texts were published in Greek, whereas the rest of the Code was to be published in Latin. Justinian, who loathed the language of Homer and pretended to be incapable of speaking it, himself explained the paradox away by saying that the texts should be understood by all.

This new code's most striking feature was the fact that it introduced Christianity into the law. Even in the preamble it rejects the various heresies and enjoins all citizens to abide by the ecclesiastical guidance of the Roman Church. There were also a number of texts governing the status of the metropolitans, the bishops, abbots and monks. A special decree authorized bishops to visit prisons, at their own discretion, in order to protect condemned and the convicted prisoners against possible abuses of the law.

Emancipated slaves henceforth were considered as enjoying all the privileges of free men, even the right to become senators or emperors.

Justinian encouraged the emancipation of slaves. The reader of the new code discerns a distinct Stoic or Christian influence in the clauses concerning the slaves. Rape of a slave woman, for example, was punishable by death, as would be the rape of a free woman. These texts also foreshadow, in a sense, the serfdom of the Middle Ages. Any free man who had cultivated a plot of land for thirty years was obliged, as were his descendants, to remain perpetually attached to that land. If he fled or become a cleric, he could be hunted down just like a fugitive slave.

Major improvements were made in the status of women. As early as the 4th century they had not been wards of their husband for their entire lives... The ancient principle whereby succession could be legitimate only through the male was definitively abandoned. Moreover, under the influence of the Church, Justinian tried to prohibit divorce, except in cases where one of the partners entered a monastery. This provision ran into a great deal of opposition in the light of prevalent custom; it was argued that the Emperor's decision would lead to a rise in the number of poisonings. In a number of subsequent texts Justinian reversed his earlier position somewhat and allowed divorce on a variety of grounds.

The penalties prescribed by Augustus for celibacy and childless marriages

were abolished. While the death penalty still applied to adultery by men, as ordained by Constantine, women, on the other hand, risked no more than internment in a religious house if they were found guilty of marital infidelity.

As for rape, the culprit was put to death and the victim received all his property.

Homosexuality was also subject to the death penalty, preceded by torture, mutilation and public display. For example, during the reign of Justinian, two bishops who had committed sodomy were castrated in public and then executed.

On the other hand it was prohibited to castrate those servants who were intended to act as guardians of the virtue of girls and women.

This legislation, which is very severe in respect of certain sexual acts, shows quite clearly the influence of Christianity with its phobia of the "sins of the flesh", as a reaction against the naturalistic morality of the pagan world.

The inheritance laws were completely changed. Previously, in the case of intestate deaths, the legal heirs were relatives on the male side, whereas now the heritage passed straight to the heirs, whether children or grand-children, with no distinction as to sex.

The property of the Church was declared to be inalienable. This, of course, was the main cause of the subsequent wealth of the Church,

A property boundary-stone being laid. Right: an official visiting a peasant.

which was thus obliged, in a sense, to accumulate property, gifts, legacies, etc., without ever being able to dispose of them. Another aspect of the influence of the Church in legal matters was the provision whereby debtors in default could be released against a bond or on oath to be present on the day of their trial.

No-one could be put in prison unless a judicial authority had issued a writ for the purpose, and preventive detention was strictly limited. Lawyers had to swear on the Bible that they would loyally defend their clients but that they would drop their advocacy if they found a person's cause to be dishonest. Judges were given broad powers of discretion in the application of penalties, and could reduce them, in particular, for women, minors and... drunks.

While preventive detention was in use under certain circumstances, confinement was rarely authorised as a penalty. Mutilation was permitted, although this represented a distinct step backwards from the codes of Hadrian or Antoninus the Pious; it suggests an oriental influence. Forgers, tax officials

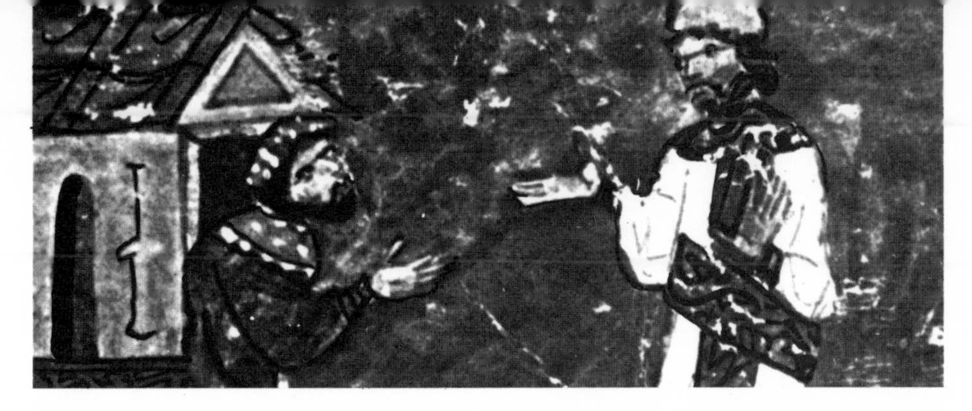

caught with their hand in the till, persons copying Monophysite texts could be sentenced to have their fist chopped off, by virtue of the Christian principle whereby the guilty member of the body should be eliminated. Amputation of the nose was the penalty for numerous offenses. Later on, the law was to prohibit the blinding of aspirants to the throne. It is true that the number of relatives of the emperors whose eyes had been gouged out was enormous.

Free men were executed by decapitation, crucifixion being reserved for slaves. As for deserters, they suffered the same fate as witches: they were burnt alive.

Any condemned person could appeal to a higher court; if that failed he could go on to the Senate and, in the last resort, appeal to the Emperor.

To the modern reader, many of the provisions of Justinian's Code must seem highly barbarous. In order to judge such matters, however, one must view them within the context of the age. An accusation often made against Justinian is that certain individual clauses in his legislation served to codify superstition and barbarity. This is an unjustified reproach, because no one man, whoever he may be, can escape from the moral environment of his age. Moses himself dictated certain laws which strike us today as sheer barbarity. On thing that can be said about our age is that, though abundantly equipped with excellent principles, it is reluctant to put them into practice. It is easier to cast anathema at earlier periods than to try to reform science. The parable of the mote and the beam is eternally valid.

Generally speaking, the Code of Justinian is praiseworthy. For generations to come, it provided order and security for an assembly of peoples with highly diverse customs. Through this code, freedom and security of communications were assured in regions where, today, despite the intervention of a host of international assemblies with their various titles, insecurity, piracy, poverty, war and death are prevalent.

The Code of Justinian, as later revived by the jurists of Bologna, gave the Western World, from the 12th century, the foundations of its civil and administrative law. As Fokrovskij rightly observes: "...it was through Justinian that Roman law revived and reunified the world a second time".

In 535 Justinian issued two decrees which gave the officials of the Empire a set of principles on which their administration was to be based. The greater part of his administrative reforms is contained in these two texts.

The revolt at Nika in 532 had shown the emperor that the common people were tired of the demands being made on them by officialdom. During the six days the revolt had lasted, rampaging mobs had been in virtual control of Constantinople, looting and burning as they went. Despite the dismissal of two ministers whom the people found particularly hateful, Tribonian and John of Cappadoccia, the rebels had not calmed down. For a while Justinian had seen power slipping out of his hands altogether, and it was only the unbending will of his wife that helped him to recover his resolve and overcame the cowardice of his companions. It was only at the last moment that General Belisarius, his courage rekindled by the attitude of the empress, reversed the situation by encircling the rebels in the Hippodrome. 30,000 of them had to be massacred in order to consolidate the power of the Empire.

Justinian knew that he had come within an inch of calamity. Although the repression he had ordered succeeded in ending the effects of the mutiny, the underlying causes still remained... The emperor now turned his intelligence, with the aid of his wife, to those causes, in full awareness that the existing administrative system and the conduct of the officials had lain at the origin of the crisis which had almost brought the State to its knees.

By means of his two *Novella* of 535, which he completed in following years, Justinian undertook the reform of the civil service of his day: many superfluous posts were simply abolished, the salaries of many officials were increased, because—as often happens in our so-called "modern" States—it was often the most useful employees who received the lowest pay. Moreover, the Byzantium of his day was teeming with newly created administrative structures in which the officials held virtual sinecures. Justinian put an end to this scandalous state of affairs. He also required all those who served the State to take an oath at the moment of their admission to the service: it does, in fact, seem curious to imagine a civil servent who could be the enemy of the system which employs him. A body of agents known as the "Justinians" was formed; these were persons, reporting directly to the Emperor, who had certain civil and military powers. Later, in the West, Charlemagne also created what he called the "*Missi Dominici*".

What this meant was that the administration was becoming centralised, and the authority of the State consequently strengthened. However, be-

The Byzantine eagle (Mistra).

sides these purely technical measures, Justinian demanded of his officials equity, justice, honesty and even Christian charity. Pursuing this end, the Emperor did away with corruption in the holding of office; unfortunately, he was later to reverse this fine principle as the State, hard pressed for cash as a result of wars and public works, began once more to sell posts in the public service, thus striking a fatal blow at an effort at administrative reform which had begun so very well. As in the past, the tax-collector was made personally responsible for the collection of taxes, a move which opened the door wide to the kind of dishonesty and excesses which Justinian had tried to end. The taxpayer, on whom the most extreme demands could be made, had nowhere to turn for protection but to the large landowners whose power Justinian had tried to break. This led to a strengthening of the privileged landowning class in its relations with the central authority. Having failed, through lack of perseverance and will-power, to carry through his reform, Justinian thus helped bring about a state of affairs which was very harmful to the Empire.

Despite his mistakes Justinian I the Great was a true Roman emperor. While preserving the Empire from the barbarian hordes, he actually carried the war into their lands, winning vast tracts of territory back for the Empire. It was thanks to his western policies that it proved possible to keep the flame of civilisation alight in certain scattered regions of Europe. Hagia Sophia was also the work of Justinian, since he restored, enlarged and embellished it.

When he died, Antiquity could truly be said to have ended too. He was the last of the Romans.

αροτηρ

5/Byzantine Society

Byzantium was a highly hierarchical society. The nobility was eloquently known as the "powerful ones". And powerful they certainly were. They were divided into a warrior aristocracy and an administrative aristocracy, which were not without their internal squabbles. The civil nobility was naturally resident in Constantinople, while the provinces were shared out among the military. Rich officials tended to buy land, while landowners centered their ambitions on getting a high post in Constantinople. A certain amount of to-and-fro resulted.

Throughout its history the Byzantine Empire was marked by the struggle between the emperors and the large landowners, who sought to expand their possessions. There were several reasons for this: firstly, it was essential to prevent the emergence of a source of power which could rival that of the emperors. During the reign of Basil II the revolt of two great lords, Bordas Skleros and Bordas Phocas, placed the imperial position in grave jeopardy. It then became necessary to defend the poor peasants, who where hard put to it to protect their pitiable plots of land, and often had to seek the shelter of a more powerful neighbor, thus losing a measure of their freedom.

Apart from anything else it was against the interest of the Treasury to

Left: a plowman and a craftsman, as seen in the Oppiano Manuscript. Above: other craftsmen.

have large tracts of land concentrated in a few hands. The tax system was so arranged that lower taxes were levied on large estates than on small holdings taxed separately. This meant that the revenues of the State declined as the properties of the great landowners expanded.

It was Romanus Lecapenus who, in an edict issued in 922, struck the first blow. He denied the powerful landowners the right to buy land from the poor, and gave preference to the peasants when there was any competition for a given piece of land. It made it compulsory to hand back confiscated or purchased military property to its legitimate owner.

In 995 Basil II enacted similar legislation: he abolished the 40-year statute of limitations which applied to purchases made by the powerful, prohibited patronage and revived a measure whereby the lord was obliged to pay for the poor if the latter was prevented from doing so himself.

Similar measures were imposed on the monasteries, which were amassing vast fortunes. Indeed, this was one of the reasons for the iconoclasm of some of the emperors.

In practice, however, all these measures came to nothing. Nothing stopped the landed aristocracy from expanding and governing an entire people of settlers, serfs and slaves.

For a long time Byzantium was a flourishing city. As long as its currency remained stable, the golden *nomisma* was in great demand in all the markets, not just in Europe but as far away as Ceylon.

Left: work in the fields. Above: the creation of the animals (Mosaic from Saint Mark's Basilica, Venice). Below: miniature taken from an XI century manuscript about hunting and fishing.

Byzantium was faithful to the kind of strictly managed economy which had been adopted ever since Constantine came to power in order to ensure regular supplies for the city. The work of craftsmen and indeed of all private labor was highly organised and regulated–though this meant establishing a huge civil service solely for the purpose. The unfortunate merchants often resented the weight of supervision which was imposed on them. For example, each morning, the prefect was the one who set the price of fish. Traders' profits could not exceed 16-17% of the net price. The silk trade was subject to numerous controls and regulations, both in order to guarantee the quality of production and to prevent any speculation. From the raw silk to the actual sale of the dyed product, there were five intermediaries to reckon with, and a host of authorisations were necessary. The quality, however, was undeniably good.

The main basis for the prosperity of the city was its superb geographical situation. Constantine had certainly made a sound choice of site for his new capital: from China the caravans brought silk to Antioch and the cities on the outer limits of the Empire. On the Red Sea, Eilath and Kysma (near modern Suez) received all the mer-

Reproduction of a miniature from the Oppiano Manuscript.

chandise from Africa–ivory, myrrh and incense– and also that coming from southern Asia and India. The ports nearer Central Europe, in the Crimea, Kherson, Bosporos and Petra, were the ports where amber and furs were unloaded. All this merchandise was easily transported to Constantinople where a large market awaited.

At the end of the 9th century, and despite the Arab threat, trade with the ports of the Mediterranean basin reached a new peak; this was particularly true of Italy, which abounded with great and fearless navigators.

It was during this period that a real luxury industry came into being in Byzantium, where fabrics and silks of exceptional quality were manufactured. Carpets and work in precious metals were especially noteworthy. Constantinople exported metal objects, ciboriums, goblets, silver ewers and similar items, often embellished with precious stones and the marvellous enamels on bronze which soon became famous everywhere.

Starting around the year 1200, however, the economic situation began to deteriorate. First, State protection for labor was gradually abandoned. The rise of Venice, however, was the really serious obstacle facing Byzantine trade routes. The Venetian occupation of Crete, Coron, Modon,

A view of the walls of St. Irene, Istanbul.

Repairs being carried out a ship. Right: Byzantine houses.

etc., enabled it to keep a close watch on Byzantine shipping and even to exclude it altogether. The emperors found themselves obliged to buy the neutrality of the numerous enemies of the Empire by means of economically disastrous treaties. The alliances of Venice, Genoa and Pisa against the Sicilian Normans were bought in this way. When Alexius Comnenus appealed to Venice for help, he had to grant all sorts of privileges: Venetian merchants were henceforth allowed to buy and sell anywhere in the territory of Byzantium without paying either import or export taxes. Their ships paid no berth fees while standing idle in harbor at wharves specially reserved for them. Such a state of affairs could not fail to be detrimental to local business.

The establishment of the Franks in Syria was to inhibit Constantinople's economic expansion even further. Oriental products now arrived directly at the gates of the Levant; the city was to find itself shoved aside from the mainstream of international trade.

Quite apart from that, Constantinople, new weakened by endless internal squabbles, was fully engaged in a desperate fight against the Turks.

The role of Constantinople as a business center was well and truly over.

There was little unity among the va-

rious classes of society as far as accomodation was concerned. The rich citizen had a two-story house, its façade adorned with multi-colored decorative work, usually in stucco. It had corbelled arches, and the windows, which consisted of small panes of glass, had a grill outside. The door was made of solid iron, opening from the center, and was heavily embossed. The roof served as a terrace.

As we enter the main door, we find ourselves in a large room as tall as the building itself with fine mosaics on the floor and frescoes on the walls. Around the room stands a marble colonnade which supports the upper floor where the bedrooms and living quarters are located. Of course, these were the dwellings of the aristocracy and the upper middle class.

Behind these luxurious houses, whose marble or porphyry porticoes were aligned according to the plans of Constantine the Great for these exclusive areas, narrow streets wound their way between ancient, crowded buildings where small businessmen and craftsmen lived one on top of another —those of them, that is, who could afford to have living quarters separate from their stall or workshop.

In such quarters the kitchen was the main room. In winter, the wood-burning fireplace often served as a bed.

Reconstitution of the façade of a classical Byzantine house. Facing: construction work.

The better-off members of this class of society had real beds with headboards at either end. The poorer would simply lie on the floor on a crude bed of straw or some similar material.

Although oil was very expensive and was always used sparingly, a tiny lamp used to burn day and night before the icon in one corner of the room.

Peasants lived in cramped and very rudimentary quarters. The more well-to-do among them had a first floor for themselves, leaving the ground floor for their animals. Barns, cellars and storage space were separate.

Family life was important in Byzantium.

The Byzantine child stayed with his mother until he was seven or eight, and she taught him the rudiments of the alphabet. Those families who could afford to do so used to hire a tutor for about three years to teach the child to read and write. For most people education never went further than that. Sometimes, however, young men took their studies on to higher levels. "Secondary" education, which lasted from seven to eight years, consisted of the study of the classical authors, with special emphasis on Homer. The methods used where highly scholastic, involving huge amounts of rote learning.

At the age of sixteen young men who belonged to the business community usually followed their father's profession, and went to work in his workshop or stall, while noble young men chose the military career and, from that vantage point, tried to find a well-endowed rich young heiress.

It was possible to carry one's studies even further, and indeed necessary to do so if one planned to be an official, doctor or lawyer, these being professions for which a diploma of higher studies was required. The doors of the University opened at this point.

According to tradition, it was Constantine the Great who founded this university. At the beginning of the Byzantine Empire the teaching of Latin language and literature was predominant. Then the tolerant Theodosius II admitted a large number of pagan professors. Under Zeno (477-491) these were accused of propagating the neo-Platonic doctrines. They were therefore made to convert or resign. Justinian renewed this ban and extended it to those professors "who have foundered in heresy". He surrounded himself, not with soldiers and eunuchs, but with men of letters and scholars who gave him the idea of entirely reorganising the structure of the university. From the very beginning of this endeavor, however, a conflict broke out between the two most famous scholars involved, Xiphilinus and Psellus. The former wanted the new university to be devoted solely to the study of law, while the latter was equally vehemently attached to the study of letters and philsophy. Constantine IX wisely reconciled them by dividing the university into two schools, one of law and the other of philosophy.

Theodore Prodromos, a Byzantine chronicler, complained about the conduct of the students who, in his opinion, were often late for class or failed to attend classes at all, choosing instead to spend their time in the arms of ladies of easy virtue. They were also lured by the theater. According to the same author, students were supposed to take notes during the class on tablets and then take part in a debate after the lecturer had finished speaking. The trouble was that they often did nothing and spent the time chatting amonst themselves, so that when the lecturer, in despair, left the room a great howl of joyous laughter went up from the assembled students.

Besides lay studies there was ecclesiastical teaching also. Though this was initially for seminarists who were preparing to enter the priesthood, in the 11th century the Church added to the classical study of theology the study of rhetoric and philosophy. This

Right: a teacher. Below: motif from a mosaic (Ravenna).

gradually led to the emergence, apart from the official university, of a free patriarchal university, where secular authors were studied in addition to the sacred writings. This institution, placed under the direction of twelve professors chosen from the most eminent figures associated with Hagia Sophia, eventually acquired considerable authority and came to approach the status enjoyed in the Middle Ages by the Sorbonne in France.

The method used by the "good fathers" of the period remind one very much of Montaigne's description of college life in France in the 16th century. With the same kind of exaggeration as we find in the author of the "Essais", Nicolas Mesirates writes: "The teachers these days are very quick to reach for their stick and take cruel pleasure in flogging the children on the back with an ox-nerve".

As was to be expected, the two branches of learning, lay and religious, were not on very cordial terms, to put it mildly. The invasion of the crusaders, which marked the end of Greek culture in Constantinople, was to reconcile them: neither of them survived the conquest of the Frankish knights, those new barbarians from the north.

ЛАЗАР
ПРИТЧА ЗА БОГАТАГО
И НИЩАГО ЛАЗАРА

6/Public holidays, entertainment, pleasure

No eastern civilisation is without its festivities, and Byzantium was no exception. The people, who had inherited the Roman fondness for games, just loved to have fun and stroll along at a leisurely pace. They readily mixed games of pagan and Christian origin; with their innate sense of stately occasion, they seized eagerly upon every opportunity which came along to indulge their love of pomp, festival, and celebrations.

The accession to the throne of a new emperor was one such occasion for public merry-making. The Basileus performed an important representative function. Resplendent in purple robes, and heavily adorned with jewels like some pagan idol, he would walk or ride slowly and majestically into the city, maintaining as solemn a pose as possible. Pulcheria, the elder sister of Theodosius II, trained her brother for the throne and spent long hours teaching him poise and self-control. The child was taught to hold a god-like composure and stay perfectly still for hours on end, as a preparation for the lengthy public ceremonies he would have to attend. The trouble with her coaching was that she taught him precious little else about the art of kingship.

To complete the public delirium on the occasion of the presentation of a new emperor, there was a distribution of coins.

The triumphs, which were copied from ancient Rome, were also magnificent and lavish ceremonies. Lengthy preparations were made, the city was swept clean, sawdust was spread out on the ground and houses and monuments were decorated with flowers. Stands were erected and were draped in fabrics of brilliant colors.

The procession would enter by the Golden Gate. The Senate and the aediles went to meet the emperor, to hand him a crown of gold and laurel, to the accompaniment of fanfares of trumpets, against a background of brilliant standards waving in the breeze. The streets were full of the joyous citizenry. Then came the army, preceded by a procession of booty and prisoners of war. If it was felt that there were not enough captives, extras were quickly rounded up in order to create a better impression!

An extraordinary triumph was offered during the reign of Justinian the Great to the famous general Belisarius, first chief of the army since the end of the Republic to receive honors hitherto reserved for emperors alone. He walked from the Hippodrome to the palace, preceded by a vast crowd of prisoners—real ones, this time!—

Byzantine fresco from a church in Bulgaria showing a banquet.

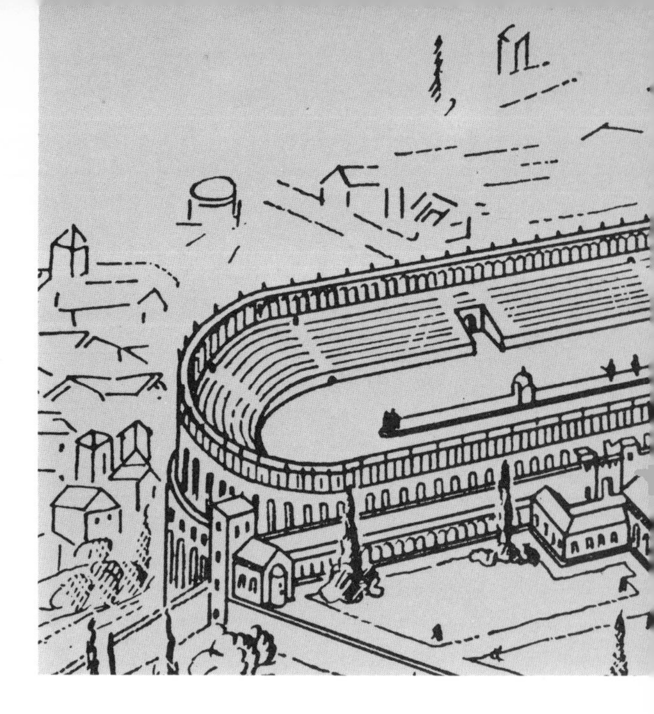

by a multitude of chariots, golden thrones, precious furniture and all the treasure of the kings of Africa. His illustrious vaniquished opponent, King Gelimer, was also there, dressed in purple and surrounded by his entire family. The ceremonies lasted for two whole days.

The occasion was a brilliant success which did much to consolidate Justinian's power for years to come.

Another spectacular event was the chariot races, held in the colossal Hippodrome which we have already described. Certain races were held on fixed dates, such as the anniversary of the founding of the city, while others took place to celebrate happy events such as a victory, the reception of some foreign dignitary, etc. Again, preparations lasted several days. First the horses themselves had to be rigorously selected and inspected. The order of the chariots at the start of the race was decided by the drawing of lots. The entire city could tell how the races were going by the clamor of the spectators and also by a veil which was hoisted to the top of the tower above the main entrance.

Thirty thousand citizens sat on the marble steps, without any special order, but after a lengthy wait outside the gates. Most people used to take their food along with them, because

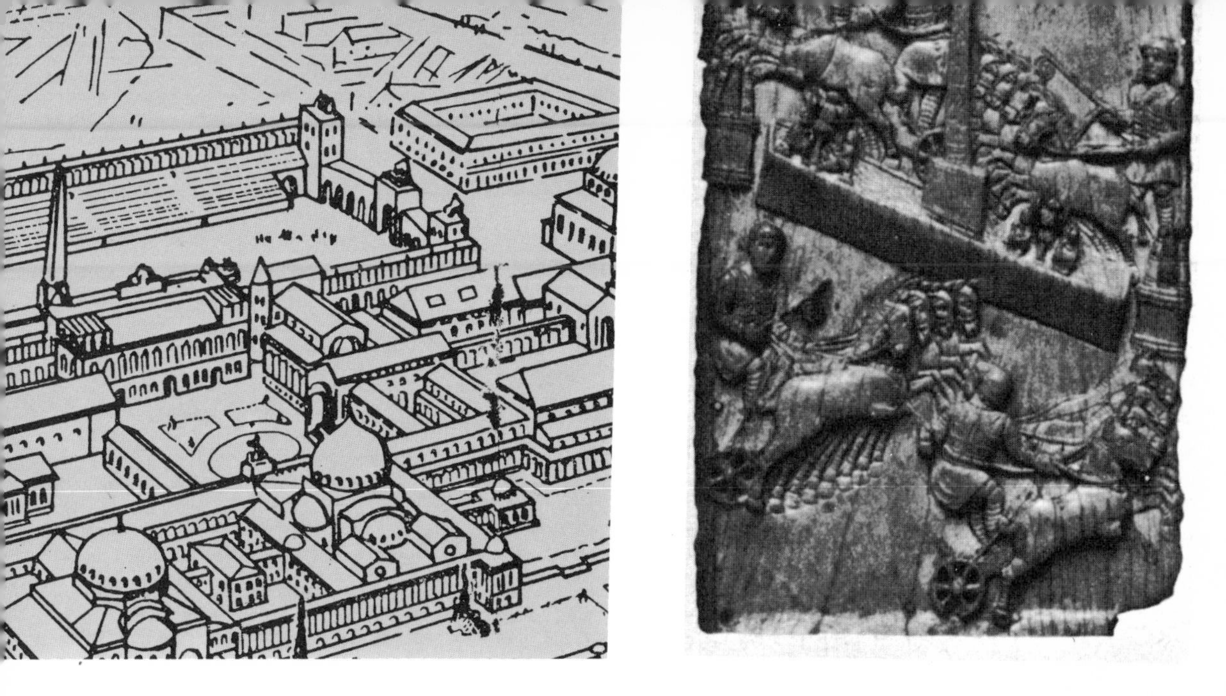

Reconstitution of the stadium of Byzantium. Above and lower left: the circus games. Lower right: the emperor and his dignitaries attending the games.

the spectacle lasted all day.

The sovereign made his solemn entry into the Hippodrome, and blessed the prostrate public three times before taking his seat in his special box. The dignitaries then entered with almost equal pomp and ceremony, and, after saluting the emperor, sat down around him. Then the sovereign dropped a piece of fabric in the arena, thus marking the beginning of the day's events. At this point the crowd exploded in a great outburst of joy, shouting and waving—sometimes, as we have seen, demonstrating their opposition to the government!—and so on until nightfall.

The races were between four quadrigas, and the horses, covered in ribbons, did seven laps of the track. Four races were held in the morning and four in the afternoon, with a long lunch break, during which the emperor withdrew to his quarters, behind the royal box. The crowd, meanwhile, remained in the stadium, unpacked their provisions and, according to custom, ran down to the track where salted fish, dried or fresh fruit and other refreshments were offered for sale. A great amount of drinking went on on such occasions. So as not to interrupt the celebrations, assorted variety shows took place on trestles erected in front of the royal box: jugglers, performing or simply rare animals, acrobats, dancers, etc. Short sketches were also played, which were often distinctly bawdy if not obscene.

The common people also had their own entertainments, of a more spontaneous sort. Torchlight processions were held on the slightest pretext. On each public square there were strolling buffoons vociferously seeking the attention of the passers-by. Besides this, there were also fortune-tellers, fetish-vendors and parades like those which occur in many modern fairgrounds.

The theater was also available. Among the several theaters in Constantinople was the Great Theater, built by Septimus Severus. All of them were open-air, and had seats arranged in stone tiers. Like their counterparts in the Commedia dell'Arte, the actors embroidered on classical themes or canvases, adultery being a frequent theme of their plays. The men and women—female roles were played by women—relied heavily on costume and were not masked. Sometimes, with unparalleled realism, they stripped off and even fornicated on stage when the script so required. Call it Hard Core, if you like!

The Church, anxious to attract the attention of the people, had another sort of entertainment to offer. It is

Byzantine figures venerating an effigy of the Virgin.

true that the spectacle was somewhat different, but the clergy had realised that ceremonial and entertaining spectacle could not fail to heighten religious fervor.

The Byzantine clergy, who had collected a prodigious amount of relics, organised grand assemblies at which the gaping public were offered, according to their choice, the swaddling clothes of the Infant Jesus, all the clothes worn by Christ on the day of the Passion—in fragments, however—, the head of St. Matthew, the teeth of St. Philip, the olive branch from Noah's Ark, one or more of the trumpets of Jericho, and a variety of other objects, each more sacred than the last.

Short sketches, like the medieval mystery plays, were acted to convey an edifying tale to the public, explaining the history of these relics and exalting their powers.

Since Arius, the mass had become a very attractive spectacle. The liturgy had become a sort of pantomime, and the canticles were entoned with a pleasant rhythm and drawing upon popular melodies of the day. Sermons were a special art-form entrusted to various persons and to choirs. For even greater effect, the members of the clergy—who were distinctly amateurish in some respects!—were sometimes replaced by professional actors, singers and producers for these

Below and right: artist's impression of offerings and a banquet-table. Following pages: Byzantine dress.

pious tasks.

Yet the popular preference definitely went to the secular festivals which had their origins in paganism, especially the festivals of the seasons, the most splendid of which was the feast of St. John which marked the beginning of summer, the day after the June solstice. Bundles of hay were set alight and people leapt through the flames; it was thought that the best jumpers would have good luck throughout the rest of the year.

The grape festival was an opportunity for vast consumption of alcohol and the holding of games rather like those of Dionysos and Bacchantes. The winter Calends were celebrated from Christmas to January 6, with a giddy round of banquets, dancing, masked parties, singing and assorted entertainments lasting days at a time, during which everyone forgot all their cares. The ecclesiastical authorities naturally took a dim view of such forms of merry-making based on pagan rites, but could do little about them and eventually gave them a Christian context.

It is obvious that the Byzantines were a jolly people. Another virtue of theirs was their love of good food. When they could afford it, even ordinary artisans and peasants indulged their fondness for excellent cooking.

The emperor set the example by holding the most sumptuous receptions. There were three dining rooms in the palace, but State banquets were held in the special chamber known as the Triclinos, with nineteen couches. Each of these couches, arranged in two rows of nine, with that of the emperor on a raised dais at one end, could accomodate twelve persons.

The basement of the palace, as was the case at Hagia Sophia, the Patriarch's domain, contained well-stocked wine-cellars and huge tanks in which provisions, and more particularly fruits, were kept cool.

For the main dish, every day, fish was served, but with incredible refinement, diversity and luxury: gigantic mullet, chrysophrys prepared in any of a thousand ways, succulent sturgeon, huge sole, boiled or fried, redfish, limanda stew. Then came caviar, served less lavishly, it is true, but generously even so. Also a variety of fish such as sea-perch, tuna, and, at the lower end of the social scale, mackerel. Lobster was also served, as were crayfish and shrimps, mussels and oysters—cooked.

Meat formed the second dish: pork, beef, mutton, venison made into stews or marinated. This latter mode of serving was highly popular in Byzantium, but it was expensive.

Theodore Prodomos gives a long list of the ingredients used by the cooks and housewives of his day: pepper, cumin, caraway, honey, nard, olive oil, vinegar, garlic, onions, mustard, cloves, cinnamon... The vegetables: cabbage, mushrooms, celery, leeks, aubergines, turnips, endives, spinach, chick peas. From their diversity it can be seen that vegetables were far from neglected.

The Byzantines also loves sweet things: fruits, fresh or dried, grapes (naturally), but also melons, apples, pears, pomegranates, figs, dates, almonds were all common items in the Byzantine dessert; they also made pastries from honey and wheat flour. They were also familiar with cheese and other dairy products. There was a choice of wines, though the sweet wines from Samos, Cyprus or Crete were preferred.

During the Macedonian dynasty, it became customary in the higher reaches of society to sit on chairs with backs around a table covered with a cloth of fine linen, using a napkin and an abundance of tableware. Drinking cups were made of tinted glass and were often mounted on a base of precious metal. Finger-bowls were a must.

The poor took their meals from a bowl in the middle of the table, and

Left: young people from Byzantium. Right: one of the cupolas of the Cathedral of Hagia Sophia. Following pages: Byzantine dress.

1
2
3
4
5
6
7
8
9
10
11
12
13
14
15
16
17
18
19
20
21

ΔΙΚΑΙΟϹΥΝΗ

1
2
3
4
5
6
7
8
9
10
11
12
13
14
20

fed largely on tuna, dried mackerel, onion soup, cheese and dried fruit.

Even so, they had three meals a day. It certainly seems that the gastronomic art was a constant concern of the Byzantines, who so keenly appreciated all the pleasures of life.

We might add that, in order to make these feasts even more delightful, Byzantines loved to get dressed up. A traveller who visited Constantinople during the reign of Manuel Comnenus reported that all the inhabitants "looked like princes, they were so well dressed".

Byzantium was a place where the ancient styles of dress took a long time to disappear. The tunic, long or short, a full, draped cloak, part of which women used to put over their heads when going out, were favorite modes of theirs. The fabrics, however, were of linen or silk among the richer members of society, even though the peasants may have gone about in a coarser cloth.

Leo the Wise lifted the ban on the use of materials which had been dyed purple, a color which had always been reserved for emperors alone. Such fabrics were then used in strips of different widths sown onto the tunic.

New series of styles of dress from Byzantium.

Under Arabian influence, the buskin was gradually replaced by soft leather

boots. Later on, the Crusaders were to introduce a fashion for hose and for closer-fitting garments in general.

Women continued to adopt the traditional hair-style: bangs on the forehead and cascading curls over the ears. Male hair-styles, however, were more varied. The emperors set the fashions, which consisted of short hair and shaved cheeks, as in the time of Julian, or full beard and long hair— sometimes very, very long — but always well groomed. Those who had not been favored by Nature wore wigs. The Byzantines knew how to use make-up and dyes. The equipment of any pretty woman included kohl, black pencils, lipstick and all sorts of perfumes.

The jewelry of Byzantium, highly ornate clusters set in gold, with precious stones ivory or enamel, was exquisitely beautiful, and a true work of art. A detail from a mosaic in the church of San Vitale at Ravenna shows us Empress Theodora wearing a tiara with numerous pendants of precious stones; her shoulders are covered with a breastplate of diamonds and necklaces.

Fine dress was an integral part of the festive occasions of Byzantium, whose citizens were persons of taste who loved luxury and the arts.

Life in Byzantium: a family outside their home, a young peasant and the ladies of the court.

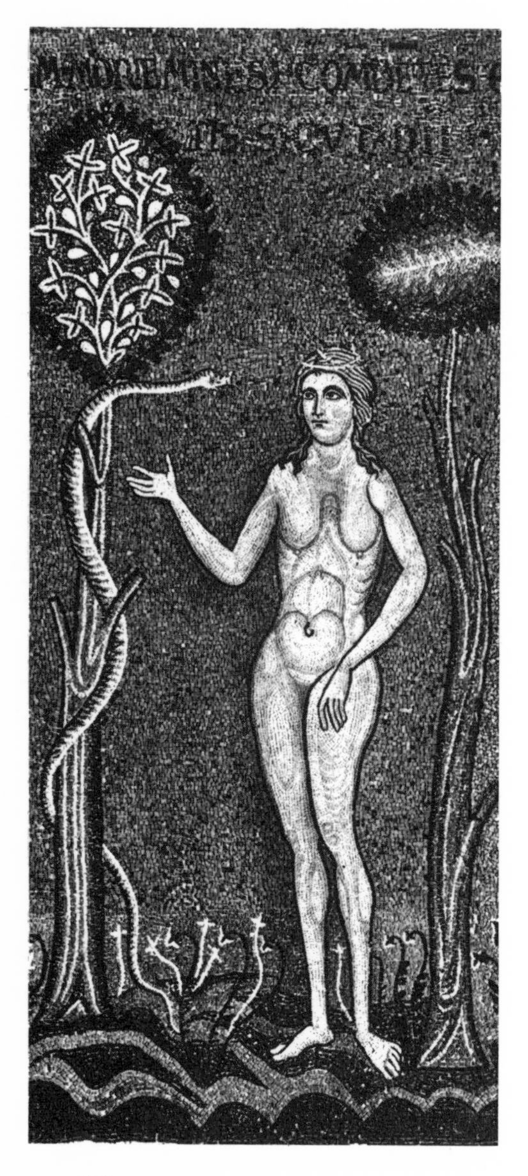

COMEDIT·DEDIT

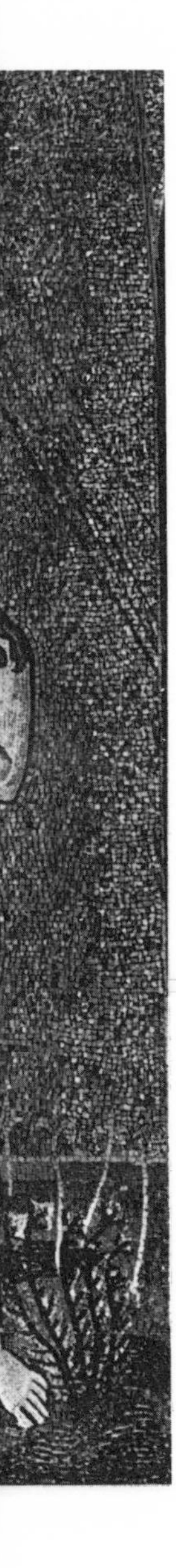

Byzantine women had an important place in society, at all levels. At least from the period of the Comneni onwards, they did not live as recluses, in the oriental manner: instead, they were very free. They were flirtatious, clever, sophisticated, ambitious, and, by all accounts, amorous, with a quick temper. This was a rough period, with some rather brutal customs.

Rape was frequent, and abduction also. Basil I ordered the death penalty for anyone found guilty of either offense, and even extended the same penalty to their accomplices – but to no avail. When some kind of sanction was applied it usually took the form of chopping off the offender's nose.

Adultery was also very widespread, though it was punishable by death in the early period of Byzantium. Leo the Wise sought to punish it as severely as a homicide, and he ordered that the adulterous spouse, of either sex, should have his or her nose cut off. However, the law was applied with variable rigor depending on the sex of the offender: women whose nose had been cut off were shut up in a convent. But a wife whose husband's nose had been cut off was obliged to continue living with him. The advantages for the poor wife in such a situation were clear – not counting the forced good humor of the husband.

Mosaics depicting the temptation of the forbidden fruit. Right: woman weaving.

Justinian allowed divorce in certain cases:

— Natural impotence of the husband or sterility of the wife which had occurred accidentally, after the marriage.

— An attempt by one of the partners on the life of the other.

— Madness for three consecutive years.

— Absence, with no news, for five consecutive years.

— Sodomy by the husband.

— Concubinage by the husband in the conjugal residence — in such cases the husband had to hand back the dowry.

— If the woman was caught, *in flagrante delicto,* in adultery.

In order for this latter case to apply, it was sufficient for her to have spent a night away from the conjugal residence or for her to have been seen at a party or a public bath with a man. In such cases the husband kept the dowry.

It is apparent that Byzantine knew nothing of equality of the sexes. But women in that society were skilled players of the power game and were capable of matching men's deviousness with their own. As Beaumarchais put it, centuries later: "If you want to make a dull girl witty, lock her up."

This was certainly true in Byzantium, because no law and no supervi-

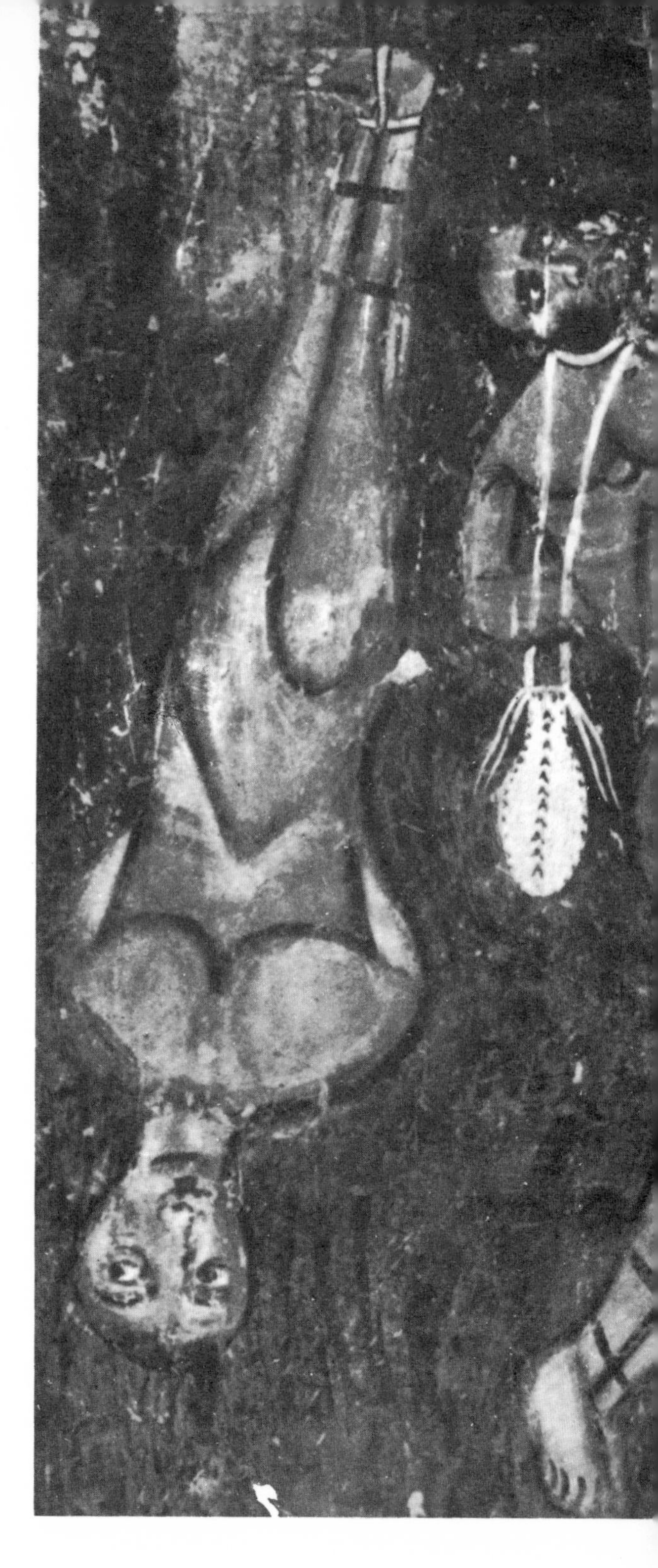

A hanged man. A saint (shunning a prostitute).

sory methods could prevent Byzantine women from cheating their husbands with a man of their choice. Eunuchs were often a useless precaution.

This oriental institution was widespread in Byzantium. It was thought prudent to entrust the protection of girls and women to a "smooth-chinned one". It should be noted, moreover, that the fact of being a eunuch was no bar to ambition; indeed, many of them sought very high office. Many of them were conspirators and some of them achieved great power. Basil, the natural son of Romanus Lecapenus, governed under three successive emperors for twenty-five years. Eunuchs often held high posts at court and could become high officials.

Prostitues formed a separate and large class of women. They practised their art in huge brothels tolerated by the administration, and they were subject to very strict tax rules, being obliged to pay one eighth of the amount paid by the customer. They accordingly were obliged to run a parallel private market. This in turn made them the prey of pimps and procurers, the "lenos" who engaged in the white slave traffic on a large scale.

A decree issued by Justinian fulminated against the doings of the "base lenos", but to little or no avail, it seems.

Figure from XI century.

Women in the upper classes could become educated and exercise a real influence. Princess Anna Comnenus, for example, was a historian who has provided us with a great amount of useful information.

Many princesses sought to act as regents or to reign themselves. Irene the mother of Constantine VI Porphyrogenitus, the last of the dynasty of the Isaurians, a woman who was given the name of "New Helen" because she restored the worship of images, reigned over the empire at a time of great upheavals, while her son was still a minor, and later reigned again after he had disappeared from the scene. In order to be rid of him she accused him of bigamy–quite likely, in view of his generally dissolute life–and then had his eyes gouged out and sent him into exile. Irene surrounded herself with ennuchs. It was even thought that the jealousy of one of them, Aece, caused the failure of Irene's marriage to Charlemagne.

One outstanding regency was that of Theodora, wife of Michael the Stammerer and mother of Michael III. She governed wisely, fought vigorously against fanaticism and conducted her foreign policy intelligently. When she left the throne in order to pass it to her son, who turned out to be a hated tyrant, she had assembled a fortune of 98,000 gold coins and 300,000 pounds of silver, which she had to account for before the State finance officers.

Some Byzantine women led very turbulent lives. For example, Zoe, daughter of Constantine VIII, was a particularly bizarre case. Having no son, the emperor had decided to marry Zoe to a patrician of his choice, Romanus Argyrus, and to name him Caesar. However, the emperor knew full well that Romanus was already married and that Zoe was fifty years old. When Romanus declined this dubious honor, the emperor gave him twenty-four hours to accept or he would have his eyes gouged out. Romanus' wife took the veil in order to disappear neatly from the scene, since she thought it more noble to save her husband's life than to share his glory. She then became empress on her father's death. Yet, despite, her age, she fell in love, not with her husband, but with a eunuch, Michael the Paphlagonian, who she appointed Chamberlain. She tried to poison her husband, but, finding the process slow, she arranged for two of her slaves to appear one evening when the emperor was in his bath and hold his head under the water until he breathed his last.

She then married her handsome

eunuch, who reigned for seven years, from 1034 to 1041, under the name of Michael IV. Having learnt from experience, and fearing his wife's ambition, Michael neutralised her by literally cloistering her in the palace. He spent his final years atoning for his faults and engaging in extreme piety. On the advice of his brother John, another eunuch, he forced Zoe to adopt his nephew Michael, who the people called the Calaphate. He then gave him the purple and the title of Caesar, had himself shaved, shut himself up in a monastery where he refused to receive Zoe's farewell and died on November 10 1041 as he was leaving the church after mass.

Michael V sat uneasily on his throne and found himself constantly threatened by Zoe's machinations. He issued a decree whereby she would be shaved and deported, but she had powerful friends who instigated a riot among the people. Despite an attempted repression in which three thousand rioters died, Michael was overthrown and packed off to a cloister—naturally, after his eyes had been gouged out!

Zoe was now in power, but, to her indignation, the Senate saddled her with a co-empress, her sister Theodora. In this way the throne was occupied by two women who hated each other

Decorative work and figures from Byzantine art, yet astonishingly modern in appearance. The same is true of the reproductions on the following pages (San Angelo in Formis).

intensely, and yet these two sisters managed to govern quite wisely for some time, contrary to general expectations.

The Senate and the common people, however, wanted an emperor, and Zoe decided to sacrifice herself by getting married yet again, while Theodora withdrew from the scene. One of her former lovers, Constantine Monomachus, was to be the new spouse. Zoe was now sixty-two years old; the reign of her husband, Constantine IX, was to be a disaster.

In 1050, Zoe died and her husband reigned for another five years, shut up in his palace with a mistress. On his death, Theodora returned from her retirement and governed wisely for two more years.

The most famous of the Byzantine empresses was the beautiful, the marvellous Theodora, wife of Justinian, who reigned from 527.

Procopius, the official palace historian, whose views should be accepted cautiously since he hated the empress, tells us that she was a woman of modest origins. The daughter of a guard at the Hippodrome, an actress and dancer by profession—and, allegedly, a courtisane when the occasion demanded. To begin with she is thought to have led a life of open debauchery in Constantinople. She was a remarkably beautiful woman, with a great deal of wit and ambition.

First, she seduced a governor of Africa who took her with him to his province and gave her a son. On her return to the capital she appeared to make a complete about-turn: suddenly she had an immense thirst for knowledge which plunged her into study and caused her to receive only scholars, magistrates and statesmen at her residence. It was at this time that she got to know Justinian, who was not yet emperor. She became his mistress "by magic powers", in the words of Procopius, though it hardly seems likely she would have needed magic for the purpose, in the light of her great beauty and charm. In any case, the love-smitten Justinian decided to marry, but the laws of Constantine and Martian prohibited marriage between senators—such as Justinian—and dancing girls. Showing unusual determination for a man who is said to have been somewhat erratic, he overcame all obstacles, wresting the necessary consent from Emperor Julian, having the laws repealed and marrying Theodora. Apparently his mother, Vigiliantia, died of shame.

Theodora was a curious and mysterious figure. She was adored by some and loathed by others, but there can be no doubt that she was generous and charitable towards the poor. She seemed a profoundly pious woman, though it was thought in some quarters that her piety was insincere. She built churches and monasteries, but persecuted the priests who would not bow to her will and the nobles who dismissed her protection disdainfully. Her companions were former whores—a fact which was interpreted variously as loyalty to former colleagues and an attempt to turn the palace into a house of prostitution. She arranged rich and noble marriages for her sisters, but also is said to have built two special prisons for the exclusive use of her personal enemies: hushed rumors went about among the populace, who called these two institutions Labyrinth and Tartar. Rumors also circulated about

Group of Virgins (mosaic and manuscript).

the disappearance of her son by her first marriage. He was thought to have displeased his mother by leaving for Africa the moment he heard about her accession to the throne. All kinds of things were being said about Theodora! Yet it is impossible to deny that she was a princess who was gifted with great finesse, breadth of mind, education and courage.

On at least one occasion Justinian owed her his throne. This was during the revolt in the Hippodrome, the so-called Nika Rebellion, which we have already described. Later on she used her influence to the full pleading on behalf of Monophysitism, and constantly urged tolerance on her husband.

Like Roman women, the women of Byzantium were nonetheless subject to male authority and, on the whole, rarely occupied the limelight.

It is interesting to recall, in this regard, the abortive conspiracy of Anna Comnenus, whose talents as a historian we have already discussed. The plot was encouraged by her father Alexius. Anna wanted her husband, Nicephorus Bryennius, a handsome, sophisticated man who already bore the title of Caesar, to accede to the throne. She intended to murder her brother John, who was not physically impressive at all, being short of stature and somewhat deformed.

However, at the last minute, whether out of fear or remorse, Bryennius refused to kill his sovereign. Anna let fly a volley of insults, claiming that "when Nature had formed the two of them, she had made a mistake, and had given her the spirit of a man". The conspiracy was discovered, and the plotters were arrested and firmly expected to be put to death. John, however, spared their lives, and merely confiscated their property, giving palace to the Grand Domestic, Axuch; he in turn refused this favor and urged John to show clemency. John then returned the confiscated properties to the guilty parties and offered an expression of friendship to his siter. This act of clemency, which thoroughly out of keeping with imperial habit, produced an immediate and lasting effect. It strengthened his power and, to compensate him for his physical shortcomings, the common people, with only his moral qualities in mind, gave him the paradoxical nickname of *Kalo* or the Handsome One.

Since this conspiracy had failed through the fault of her husband, Anna is said to have cried out in her rage: "How awful it is to have a hole instead of a penis!"

She cannot have been the only Byzantine woman to have held such views!

Ravenna mosaic depicting Empress Theodora and a minister.

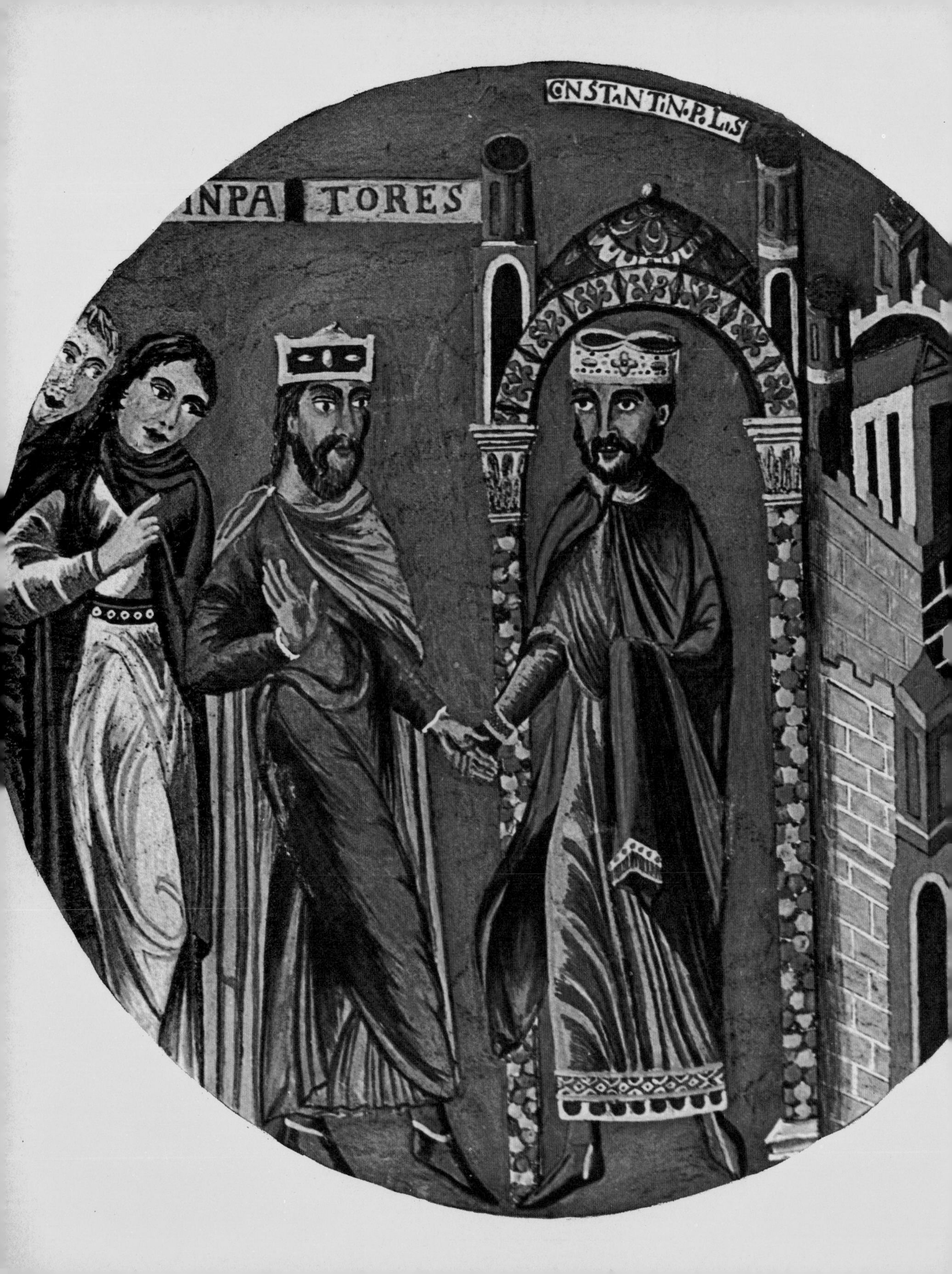

INPA TORES
CONSTANTINOPOLIS

Another eminent woman, who was also a scholar in the fullest sense of the term, and one of the most beautiful figures of the pagan world, was Hypatia, who lived in the later part of the 4th century.

Her father, Theo, was a professor at the Museum of Alexandria and she helped in his work so well that she became an accomplished mathematician and philosopher, to the point where she was appointed to the chair of philosophy at the Museum. She designed a system along Platonic lines; her courses were so eloquently delivered that students came from far and wide to attend them. She was able to discuss the most abstruse points of Plato or Aristotle with ease and hold her own against the most expert magistrates. At the same time she managed to preserve her beauty.

It was said that many students fell in love with her but that she always repelled their advances. When pestered by an importunate student, she suddenly lifted up her skirts and replied: "What you love is this impure symbol of generation, not beauty itself."

Unfortunately for her, she had to fend off the attacks of the Christians of Alexandria, and, in particular, of Archbishop Cyril, who accused her of having a bad influence on Orestes, the

Emperor Charlemagne on a visit to Constantinople (medieval manuscript).

prefect of the town who was her friend and, like her, a pagan. In 415, a band of fanatics, led by a cleric from the followers of Cyril, drew her into an ambush, dragged her into a church and then, with little regard for the sacrilege they were committing, beat her savagely, with unheard of cruelty which continued even after she was dead, as they hacked her to death and burned the poor woman's remains.

This unspeakable act of cruelty went entirely unpunished. The fact was that the Church had never particularly liked women, whom it regarded as an incarnation of Eve who had brought doom to Adam and was an instrument of the Devil.

Saint John Chrysostom, a truly Byzantine saint, who was Patriarch of Constantinople, held views concerning women which say everything: "Women are a necessary evil, a natural temptation, a desirable calamity, a domestic peril, a mortal fascination, a painted scourge."

Left: statue of the female scholar Hypatia. Right: church decoration from the Iconoclast period.

8/Religion and Byzantinism

Even though Byzantium, in the course of its history, changed from a Latin to a Greek Empire, it was at all times a Christian empire... but a disunited Christian empire which was shaken by a succession of religious conflicts. This was due to the very nature of Christianity, which, ever since its origin, had set itself a catholic, or universal mission, apostolic in the sense that it emanated directly from the apostles. With the increasing pre-eminence of the bishops of Rome, it became Roman as well. This triple conception made it a dogmatic religion, one in which only the Church Councils and the Pope could pronounce on matters of faith. This intransigence was to collide with a trend towards the free interpretation of the sacred texts; in Byzantium, which was thoroughly imbued with the analytical spirit which had been inherited from Athens, heresies abounded and their multiplicity poisoned the political life of the empire.

Long before the foundation of Constantinople the Church had been obliged to fight a number of heretical tendencies, the most important of which was *gnosticism.* But nowhere in the whole of Christendom was the confusion as great nor as harmful as in Byzantium.

Starting in 316, Donat, Bishop of

The Creation of the World (Saint Mark's, Venice).

Carthage, maintained that the only legitimate Church was that of Africa. His followers, the *circumcelliones* or the *agnostitici,* rebaptised the faithful under them. They espoused violence in the quest for martyrdom and, for the first time, made it necessary for Constantine to intervene in the internal affairs of the Church, scattering their troops who had formed themselves into bands of outlaws and looters. Even so, he did not succeed in wiping out the sect itself, which was to survive until the 6th century and offer a target for the theological thunder of Saint Augustine.

The second intervention by Constantine in ecclesiastical matters came with the Arian heresy. Arius, a priest from the district of Alexandria, had been propagating a doctrine which had originated in Syria in the 3rd century, and which denied the equality of the three members of the Trinity. Arius believed that, if God the Father was really eternal and not engendered, the Son must be a creature of the Father. This was tantamount to a denial of "consubstantiality" and, accordingly, of the divinity of Christ.

Arius was a clever public relations man who presented his doctrines in the form of canticles, thus winning thousands of followers. He was therefore vigorously excommuniated by the bishop of Alexandria, who had his decision confirmed by a synod in 321.

Arius took refuge in Palestine, but the eastern Christian world was so thoroughly divided by this dispute that Constantine decided to intervene in order to protect the civil peace. In 325 he assembled an ecumenical council, at Nicaea—in fact, the first such council. With two exceptions, the bishops agreed on the famous *Symbolum Nicenum,* or Nicaean Creed, which declared flatly that the Son was consubstantial with the Father, in other words, that they had a unity and identity of substance. This council laid the very foundations of the Catholic Church, but the question was far from settled. On this occasion the political powers intervened, not merely in connection with the crisis over bishop Donat, but on a matter of dogma. Subsequent relations between the temporal and the spiritual sectors can be traced back to this point. The temporal was then to serve as the right arm of the spiritual just after the Council of Nicaea, in arranging for Arius and his most ardent followers to be exiled to Illyria. Nonetheless, twelve years later, Constantine was baptised, just before his death, by an Arian bishop.

Constant interference occurred throughout Byzantine history between

The Eternal Life that is to come: the chosen ones and the damned (miniature from a manuscript).

the civil authority and the Church. To the mind of a modern Western reader such a phenomenon may seem strange indeed, but it was common in Antiquity and still occurs today in several oriental societies. It took numerous forms, ranging from the Hebraic theocracy to the civil Roman religion perpetuated under the Caesars by the role of the Pontifex Maximus which belonged, by right, to the emperor.

Though Constantine the Great was unwilling to regard Christianity as anything other than the privileged religion of the Empire, the same was not true of his son Constance. He had come to power by means of the systematic extermination of the members of his family, including his two brothers Constantine II and Constant. The only one to escape was a young relative, Julian, who was thought to be harmless on account of his age. Constance was not content to merely favor the religion of Christ: he persecuted paganism. He was a cruel prince who sided with the Arians against the orthodox Christians. The historian Ammienus Marcellinus spoke thus of the religious conflicts of the period: "There is no wild beast which could be a worse enemy of man than most of the Christians are towards each other."

During the reign of Constance, Julian was appointed Caesar of the Gauls, which conveniently removed him from the capital. He was an excellent general, and very popular with his men. He was a man of measured thought and action, judicious, calm and gentle; he cultivated the study of literature and, having been initiated into neo-Platonic doctrines, he saw in them a way of opposing the rise of Christian mysticism.

He had accepted the post of governor of the Gauls with extreme reluctance. "This post suits me as well as a saddle fits an ox", as he put it. Yet his prestige was steadily rising: he was proclaimed Augustus by his troops. A confrontation with Constance was therefore inevitable, but, luckily, the latter died in 361.

There was now no obstacle to the accession to the throne of the very famous emperor who was to be known as Julian the Apostate. Montesquieu had this to say of him: "By his wisdom, his constancy, his discipline, his conduct, his values and a steady stream of heroic acts, he repelled the barbarians and the terror inspired by his name kept them at bay as long as he was alive."

Julian had to leave Lutèce for his coronation. He wrote poetically about his habitual place of residence: "I shall spend the winter in my dear

Opposite: Byzantine church in Athens and illumination from a manuscript depicting a scene from the gospels.

Lutèce, which is the name given gy the Gauls to the small city of the Parisii. It is situated on an island in the middle of the river and is joined to the banks on either side by two bridges. The river rarely rises or falls. Its pure, clear water can be drunk straight out of the river, and the Parisii even manage to grow figs, covering them with straw in winter."

From the moment of his succession to the imperial throne, Julian set about realising his dream: the reconstitution of the Roman Empire, the crushing of the Persians, and the restoration of the ancient religion–it is for this reason that his enemies gave him the name Apostate. Actually, it is a misnomer, for he was never a Christian. He forbade the opening of Christian schools, in these terms: "You cannot explain secular texts if you condemn the doctrine which they contain; if you do wish to teach them then you must necessarily approve their principles." He preached religious tolerance and practised justice and the love of one's neighbor.

In the words of Montaigne: "He was a very great and very rare man, whose soul was tinged with the discourses on philosophy on which he professed to base all his actions." Besides all these qualities, he was chaste; when offered a number of beautiful captive

girls, he accepted none of them, even though he was in the flower of manhood.

This was a man from another age, and his reign did not last long. He was killed by an arrow during a battle with the Parthians in 363, at the age of 31. His death was a model of resignation. Though gravely wounded he talked to his friends, just like Socrates, till the very end, urging them not to despair, because his soul was going to merge with Nature. This was the death of a philosopher-king, such as would have pleased Plato.

Under Theodosius II Christianity became the State religion, and Arianism was banned. Emperor Gratianus had already refused the title of Pontifex Maximus and was unwilling to sacrifice to the pagan goddess of victory. Theodosius ordered the closing of the temples of the ancient gods and had their altars broken. He destroyed the pagan statues and attached bits and pieces of them, out of sheer derision, to the wheels of his chariot. An edict issued in 392 prescribed the death penalty for the worship of idols. The Serapeum of Memphis was closed, the fire kept burning by the Vestals was extinguished, the statue of Victory was removed from the Senate and the Olympic Games were abolished: the Great Pan was definitively dead.

In addition, Theodosius recognized in the Church a power superior to that of the emperor. After the massacre of the inhabitants of Thessalonika he complied with the decision of Saint Ambrose, who had excommunicated him, and agreed to confess his faults in public. What exemplary self-criticism! The spiritual now well and truly predominated over the temporal—a state of affairs which was to last for centuries in the Christian world, but which could not prevent the quarrels caused by problems of exegesis, in which the emperors were always closely involved.

Some of them came to neglect their State responsibilities altogether, preferring instead to spend their time discussing with bishops and monks on points of doctrinal detail. For example, Theodosus II, of whom we have already spoken, spent most of his reign wading ever more deeply into the mire of Christological conflict.

The Council of Nicaea had decreed as a matter of faith the double nature of Christ, man and god. Thenceforth, discussion centered on the following grave issue: how did these two natures become united in the person of Christ?

At Antioch, a patriarch of Constantinople, Nestorius, held that the two natures of Christ were quite distinct and the human nature was predomi-

An imposing God the Father (Byzantine fresco, Athens).

nant—in other words, Christ was merely a man made god.

It so happened that the bishops of Antioch envied the episcopal primacy of their counterparts in Byzantium. When the bishop of Rome, Celestin, condemned Nestorius in 428, the bishop of Alexandria, Cyril, assembled an Egyptian council and ordered Nestorius to concede. Theodosius II, who was very interested by these matters, took an active part in the proceedings. He convened a third ecumenical council at Ephesus in 431. Cyril attended it with a large body of armed followers, and by buying and threatening he won over the council, which then dismissed Nestorius. However, in order to combat the Nestorian thesis, the Alexandrians had emphasized the divine nature of Christ so forcefully, to the detriment of his human nature, that they found themselves stating the positions of Monophysitism, a doctrine which was no more orthodox than the previous one. It was also condemned by Pope Leo the Great.

As a result of this condemnation, a new council was convened at Ephesus in 449, by the same Theodosius II, whose passion for theology had not diminished one bit. This council was to be known in history under the significant title "Piracy of Ephesus". Dioscouros the successor of Cyril, had improved on his methods and succeeded in creating a climate of genuine terror, winning a condemnation of the distinction between the dual nature of Christ, which was the doctrine of Rome. Monophysitism triumphed, and the papal envoys, fearing for their lives, fled from the scene. The emperor ratified the decision of the council, thus creating a grave religious crisis which was to shake the State to its foundations...

Meanwhile, during these dramatic goings-on on the battle-fields of theology, the Christian East was being threatened by the worst of dangers: the Persians and the Arabs were threatening the Asian provinces, the Vandals of Africa were plundering the coasts, tribute was being paid to the Huns and Attila insulted the emperor.

In 451, Emperor Martian, the successor of Theodosius, seeking to put an end to these disputes, convened a fourth ecumenical council at Chalcedon—fourth, because the Council of Ephesus in 449 was not ecumenical since it had not assembled all the bishops. The papal envoys were present and succeeded in having Dioscouros deposed and Monophysitism condemned. This council was of capital importance because it laid the foundations of orthodoxy; at the hierarchical level it confirmed the authority

The Byzantine cross (Athens).

of the bishop of Rome, who thus truly became the Pope.

However, Syria, Egypt and numerous regions of Asia did not accept these decisions and were to remain faithful to Monophysitism. Rioting broke out in Alexandria and Antioch. A part of the Eastern world rose up against Byzantium.

In 482, in a praiseworthy attempt to restore peace in the consciences of men and in the State, Emperor Zeno published the Henotikon or declaration of union. Unfortunately this mediocre document did not satisfy anyone. Both Monophysites and Orthodox rejected the decree violently and Pope went so far as to excommunicate the Patriarch of Constantinople, Acacius, who had advised the emperor. In response, Acacius had the name of the Pope erased from all prayers. This marked the beginning of the First Schism between East and West; it lasted until 519. At this time, Emperor Justin, who had held lengthy and laborious negotiations with Pope Hormisdas, managed to put an end to the break with Acacius, whose death, in 489, happened to smooth matters considerably. The Patriarch of Constantinople and the majority of the Eastern bishops then signed a formula of union known as the "Hormisdas Formula", which restored the unity of the Church on the basis of the Council of Chalcedon.

The Monophysite affair was far from over, however. Its resurgence and repercussions on numerous occasions were to poison the political climate in the Eastern Empire for many years to come.

During the reign of the great Justinian a ferocious brand of orthodoxy came to be established. Severe laws were enacted against heretics. Virtue was the crucial quality of the day. Courts were supervised by bishops, married priests were denied the chance to become bishops, gambling was banned since it was felt that it gave rise to blasphemy. Two bishops found guilty of sodomy were castrated in public. On the other hand, a law was passed banning the castration of servants for use as guardians of the virtue of women and girls.

Theodora, who had not, herself, always been chaste and pure, converted a palace for use as a house of penitence for repentant prostitutes. The same empress, for strictly political reasons, maintained a strong current of Monophysitism even in the imperial palace. She had not forgotten that Egypt and Syria, the two richest provinces of the Empire, had remained faithful to that thesis. In 543, Justinian even had a council, known as the

Three Chapters, condemn the texts of the Council of Chalcedonia. He kidnapped Pope Vigil from Rome and, through entreaty and outright threats, got him to confirm the work of that council. However, when Theodora died, the Pope felt free to go back on his word.

In this way the Christian unity of the Eastern Empire was being weakened at the very time when it could have been useful as protection against Islam which was about to unleash the Arab invasion on Europe.

Under the reign of Heraclius, who attempted a reconciliation by creating a new doctrine, Monotheism, things developed to a stage where whole provinces preferred to live under Arab domination, because at least they would be enabled to practice their religion in freedom.

The loss of the Monophysite provinces gave the Empire the religious unity which it had always sorely lacked. Constantine IV restored orthodoxy. At the same time, like Antioch, Jerusalem and Alexandria had fallen into the hands of the Muslims, the eternal source of conflicts of influence between these patriarchs and the patriarch of Constantinople was about to disappear.

But the Byzantines were soon going to find other issues to debate!

The famous church of Saint Irene, Istanbul.

Leo II the Isaurian had a happy reign and fought successfully against the Arabs. Yet he too had a passion for theology and he suddenly decided that the worship of images was a mere superstition. His followers then systematically destroyed religious images–thus anihilating vast numbers of works of art–while he announced his decision to the Pope as having been taken by him as a "priest and an emperor".

He convened a council to find support for his thesis in 730; the Pope riposted by convening a counter-council. Leo tried to take his adversary prisoner, dispatching the Duke of Sibyrius for this purpose, but the citizens of Rome defended their Pope successfully. Leo was infuriated, and decided to withdraw from the jurisdiction of Rome the provinces of Greece, Illyria and Macedonia, which he placed under the authority of the Patriarch of Constantinople. The great quarrel between the Latin Church and the Greek Church began at this point.

Meanwhile, the Saracens were plundering and holding up to ransom the Empire.

In 754 a new council, at Heria, condemned the worship of images even more vehemently. Emperor Constantine V went so far as to persecute the Iconophiles, some of whom were decapitated, while the monks were constantly harassed.

It was not until 787 that a new ecumenical council, the seventh, meeting again at Nicaea, reverted to the Catholic theses. The worship of images was restored and the Iconoclasts were excommunicated. Carried away with joy, the Orthodox acclaimed the young emperor who was reigning at the time, Constantine VI, comparing him to his illustrious predecessor, the great Constantine.

The iconoclast emperors were not at all unbelievers; far from it, they were often very pious souls who sought to defend themselves against a real idolatry of images which was all too popular in the mass of the people. For them, this was also a way of reacting against the growing influence of the monks, who were proliferating at the time. The monasteries were expanding in both number and wealth, power and prestige. This state of affairs was a danger for the civil authority, and one which a man like Leo the Armenian discerned quite well.

The result of these religious disputes was a violent latent antagonism between the Eastern and Western Churches. It came to the surface in 867 when a council meeting at Constantinople anathemised Pope Nicolas I for

his "illegal" intervention in the affairs of the East. This split was to be known as the Photian Schism after the patriarch responsible for it.

A more serious and more lasting schism occurred in the 11th century as a result of an arrogant and unrelenting rivalry between a papal envoy, Cardinal Humbert, and Patriarch Michael Cerularius. After numerous incidents, Michael Cerularius, finding himself excommunicated and furious for that reason, in turn convened a council which then proceeded to excommunicate all the papal envoys.

This time a definitive split occurred between the two churches; it was an undisputed victory for the Patriarchate of Constantinople which was now liberated from subjection to Rome and enjoyed greatly enhanced prestige throughout the East.

A victory it was, certainly, but... henceforth, Constantinople was an enemy in Rome's eyes. It is conceivable that Rome might have come to the help of its faithful church when, later on, Constantinople was in need of help against the marauding Turks.

A mere hypothesis, perhaps, but who knows? If Byzantium had remained subordinate to the Pope, the face of the world might well have been changed.

Below: ornamental work from the façade of a Byzantine church in Athens, and, right, sanctuary at Mistra.

9/The Byzantine clergy

An empire in which religious problems were so prominent was obviously a Promised Land for the clergy. And the role of its chief was of capital importance.

In 381, an ecumenical council held in Constantinople gave the bishopric of that city, which was known as the "New Rome", immediate pre-eminence after Rome, thus causing immense displeasure in Alexandria, which had hitherto been the unquestioned intellectual and religious center of the East.

The Council of Chalcedon in 451 confirmed the primacy of Constantinople and the authority of its Patriarch. His authority was certainly vast. From the 6th century onwards it covered 31 bishoprics and kept growing constantly until the middle of the 11th century. It was to suffer the same fate as the Empire, being dismembered after the crusade of 1204.

The patriarch was regarded as the representative of the Church. He was "by the grace of God, Archbishop of Constantinople, the New Rome and ecumenical patriarch". In theory he was accountable only to God, but in fact, being an appointee of the Emperor, he was dependent on him.

The Emperor chose him out of three candidates presented to him by the metropolitans, assuming that one of

The Basilica of San Vitale, Ravenna.

Base of a Byzantine lectern, XI century.

the three was to his liking. If none of them won the imperial favor he rejected them all and simply appointed someone else, the man of his choice being elected *ex officio*. Being the Emperor, what he did he could also undo: a Patriarch who incurred his displeasure was as good as dismissed.

In this way, thirty-six of them were removed from office by the will of the Basileus, out of the one hundred and twenty two who succeeded each other in the post. This figure does not include the large numbers Patriarchs who preferred to resign rather than await the full weight of the imperial wrath. Accordingly, the Patriarch could be said to be the Emperor's first servant, his Minister of Worship, as it were.

Even so, he was still the head of the ecclesiastical hierarchy, and wielded enormous administrative power: so much so that it often consumed all of his time. There were precious few patriarchs who were particularly noted for their spirituality. Saint John Chrysostom in 398 and Nestorius in 428 were the happy exceptions. Generally speaking, the Patriarch was above all a diplomat, a politician and a wily tactician who was often able to exercise real influence, more through skill than through authority.

The house of the Patriarch was composed of four deputies who administered the large body of staff, and of forty-five high officials.

His first associate was the Grand Chartophylax, who was the chief of the Chancellery, with control over questions of discipline regarding the secular clergy of the capital. The Grand Sacillarius had the same powers over the regular clergy. The Grand Economius was concerned with the revenues from the Patriarchat's huge properties; he also managed the finances and audited the books. But the most demanding role of was that of the Grand Skeuophylax, whose job it was to handle the Treasury and to ensure the provision of everything necessary for the celebration of the Holy Office.

The Arch-Deacon had a more spiritual role and the Referendarius was the liaison officer with the imperial palace.

The Patriarch had a sumptuous palace next to the cathedral of Saint Sophia, in which he enjoyed unquestionable luxury. He also had several country houses, vast land holdings and... a prison, kept specially for his enemies.

The priests were virtually innumerable. A census taken during the reign of Manuel Comnenus recorded 56,000 priests, 40,000 of them secular priests lived in Constantinople. The religious state was highly sought after, bepriests lived in Constantinople. The

religious was highly sought after, because of the financial advantages and the power that went with it. This was particularly true of the clergy of the capital which was attached to the Patriarchate. These were the posts for which the competition was keenest. There were 500 titular clerics attached to Hagia Sophia.

In the provinces the secular clergy enjoyed the revenues of their churches, which were sometimes very high indeed. Donations were frequent and ample. Priests were often worldly, of dissolute habits and more dependent for their advancement on deviousness and intrigues than on their spiritual capacities. They lived very well and were authorized to marry, except under certain Patriarchs who advocated sexual abstinence; even in such cases it was possible to indulge the pleasures of the flesh by finding a way around the ban.

The monks enjoyed the benefits resulting from virtually the entire real estate holdings of the Church, and were, for that reason, particularly envied. The monasteries had large estates, so large in some cases that they thwarted the plans of the emperors, who sought to keep in being a middle class of smaller landowners. In this struggle, as we have seen, the sovereigns were more often than not unsuccessful. The Basileus Nicephorus Phocas enacted a new law in 964 whereby the number and size of the monasteries and their land would be limited; but the law was never applied. As for Isaac Comnenus, who tried to raise funds by confiscating church lands, he was really ambitious! But he never came near actual enforcement of

Terrifying representation of an earthquake and portrait in mosaic of Saint John Chrysostom.

his plans and had to abdicate a month later. Rather than persisting in his efforts to beat the monks, he preferred to join them, and the growth in ecclesiastical wealth continued as before.

In Constantinople itself, whole streets were lined with religious establishments which vied with each other for magnificence even in their mausoleums; their donors were as generous as ever.

Monasteries were springing up everywhere, like mushrooms. After all, in order to found a religious house, all you needed was three people. Then the founder planted a cross on the land around the house and started building. After which the establishment of a community was an easy matter.

The community was directed by a *higumen,* the choice of which was supposed to be subject to the approval of the patriarch. It was often wealth, influence or family ties which actually decided the choice of higumen, and indeed of all the priests in general. Above all else, the higumen had to be a shrewd businessman who would make the affairs of the community prosper.

The epistemonarch, who was in charge of discipline, monitored respect for the rules, tried to eliminate laziness, gluttony and violence. Apparently, his job was not easy. His troubles were

even greater in the fight against the sins of the flesh, which was a department in which the monks were often sadly at fault.

Things were much worse in the convents. "Virginity is no longer to be found within these walls!" exclaimed one patriarch of Antioch, in dismay. The nuns certainly liked the good life. The convents readily let in gardeners and male workers who lived on the premises and spent the night there too.

As if that were not enough, "society" women often decided to retire, after the loss of a husband, for example, to a convent. But they did not intend thereby to deny themselves the comforts of the worldly life. They entertained both men and women, and had servants of either sex. The wolves were well and truly inside the sheep-pen!

Worse still, married couples often decided to withdraw together to a convent, sometimes accompanied by their children, living their ordinary communal life. In other words, it was possible to have a "private apartment" in a monastery, for reasons which had little to do with religion. Later on, as the decadence of Byzantium deepened, unmarried persons, merely living together, took to living this way, though they were bound by amorous, rather than by legal or religious, bonds. This monastic concubinage lasted for centuries, despite the determination of certain patriarchs, including, particularly, Saint John Chrysostom. These dual-purpose monasteries existed until the end of the Byzantine Empire and were more numerous the further one went away from the capital. Babies were born there, too: a really cosy family set-up!

All of this severely tarnished the religious reputation of Byzantium. However, the hermits, anachorites and saints are a better illustration of the spirituality of the Eastern Church.

A fine example of such a life is provided by Antonius, who lived in the 4th century in a minute cell on Mount Kolzim, near the Red Sea, in such a state of deprivation that he won the admiration of all who came near and taught them. He never washed and is thought to have died at the age one hundred and five.

Pacomus was also a famous hermit who founded nine monasteries in the period around the year 325, and went fifty years without ever lying down to sleep. A certain Macarius of Alexandria "could not bear to hear a description of some ascetic feat without immediately trying to surpass it", we learn from Abbé Duchesne. For example, for more than seven years, he ate no cooked food at all, and stayed awake for twenty nights in a

Detail of a crowd of men praying imploringly to Heaven.

row. He stood upright for the entire duration of Lent one year, and ate virtually nothing. A certain virgin named Sylvia refused to wash anything other than the tips of her fingers.

Simeon the Stylite was a remarkable case of such ascetic exploits. About 422, he built a column somewhere in northern Syria, and perched at the top of it. Later he built other columns, even higher than the first one, and eventually lived for thirty years at the top of a pillar 65 feet high, the surface area of which at the top had a circumference of about three feet. He attached him self to it with thick strands which soon began to cut into his flesh and cause sores to develop, to the point where his body was crawling with worms. When some of them fell off, Simeon would pick them up and put them back on his wounds, not wishing to deprive these innocent creatures of sustenance. From the top of his pedestal, to which his faithful used to hoist up some frugal fare for him to eat, he used to preach, convert and perform miraculous cures among the assembled crowd, which was full of admiration for his virtues. After a while he acquired a following among like-minded ascetics, who perched on other columns not far from his own.

While it did not encourage such excesses, the Church nevertheless derived a measure of prestige from them.

The bishops were often real politicians. It was only rarely that one found a fanatic such as Theophile, who, in 389, burned the pagan library at Serapis. On the whole, they were, fortunately, much more tolerant, good-natured men. Synesios, for example, the bishop of Ptolemais, was a paganist who was a good friend of Hypatia, the remarkable woman philosopher whom we have already described. He agreed to convert to Christianity only out of courtesy towards the Christian woman he married in 403. Moreover, it was in his capacity as a spouse that he acceded to the bishopric, without causing too much of a stir.

The Great Basil, Bishop of Cesarea, advised his flock against imitating the excesses of the anchorites and to serve God by staying healthy and preserving one's spiritual joy, which he felt was much more to the point.

The most famous of the bishops of Byzantium was Saint John Chrysostom, who became Patriarch in 398; his name derives from the Greek words for "mouth of gold", an allusion to his great eloquence. Formerly a lawyer, he entered the priesthood late in life, but with such zeal that his reputation grew rapidly. On his elevation to the Patriarchate he won great admiration

among the faithful by his goodness and charity. He had a quick mind and unmistakable authority; his preaching was an unforgettable experience to all who heard it. He vehemently denounced social injustice, immorality, high living, pleasures and pomp, and he also had few kind words to say about the theater.

He was highly unpopular with Empress Eudoxia, who took a dim view of his preaching and his scathing allusions to her debauched way of life. She managed to have him exiled to Bythynia, despite the resistance of the common people, who kept John for five days in their midst. Hardly had he gone into exile when a violent earthquake took place. Eudoxia thought it was a sign from on high, and hastily summoned her enemy back. Unfortunately, her fears evaporated shortly thereafter, and, in the face of continued Patriarchal attacks on the dissolute lives of the high and mighty, she removed him from his ecclesiastical seat once more. Under armed guard, he wandered from Nicaea to Cucusa and then reached the Euxin Bridge. The fatigue of such a journey, in the blazing heat of the sun, aggravated by the rough treatment he endured from the soldiers who surrounded him wrecked his health. The Patriarch died in 407 at Comara at the age of sixty-seven, the object of widespread veneration. He left a large body of writings, sermons, letters and treatises which are quite well known. The Church celebrates his memory on January 27.

As we have seen, Byzantine Christianity was full of contrasts: religious fervor was always accompanied by violence, brutality and crudeness. Such were the customs in this Asian world. The Byzantine Church knew only the radiant Christ,

Byzantine church (XIII century) in a small Turkish town, detail from an ornate window in Greece.

Christ the King, and not the suffering Christ, or Christ crucified.

In religious art he is always represented as a monarch, with a diadem on his head, the orb of the Earth in his hand, clad in purple and full of glory. This is far removed from the humble shepherd of early religious art. The Byzantine liturgy is thoroughly imbued with this attitude. Magnificence is the dominant feeling, the ceremonies themselves are always grandiose and sumptuous. Hagia Sophia is the dazzling symbol of Byzantine religious sentiment: sparkling with gold, precious stones, enamels, marble and mosaics, it was the scene of some splendid liturgical celebrations. It was the "Great Church of Christ", the symbol of divine wisdom of the Sophia.

The Church of Byzantium always longed to supplant Rome, and its glory lies in the extent to which it succeeded for a time in doing just that. However, after the great theological struggles, which astonished the world with the intolerance which they released, eastern monarchism began to wane. Some of the more famous monasteries devoted themselves to such a severely contemplative life that the cares of the Empire were of virtually no interest to them. The monastery of Mount Athos, which had long been at the head of Byzantine monarchism, became purely a center for meditation and mysticism, and deliberately avoided playing any role whatsoever in the government of the Church.

By the 10th century, the Byzantine Church, after the Great Schism with the West, was quite content to be the custodian of a glorious past.

10/Literature and the arts.

Byzantine literature has a dual nature–it is Greek and Christian. Its first origin left imprinted on it many features of the paganism of antiquity, whereas it also became highly doctrinal and theological, and was thus typically Christian.

The study of the Ancients was one of the foundations of education; regardless of the fervor with which they embraced their new faith, all cultivated people drew inspiration from such study. Contact with the traditions of Ancient Greece was never to disappear. Moreover, after the fall of the Byzantine Empire, it was the Greeks who, fleeing from the Ottomans, settled in Europe and brought about a renewal of Western thinking. All the works of the Ancient Greeks, which had been forgotten during the Middle Ages when Greek had been regarded as virtually an accursed tongue, were to be studied once more. While the Middle Ages was quite familiar with Latin literature, its knowledge of Greek literature was slight indeed. After all, this was the language of the great heresies, the language of Nestorius, Arius and Eutyches. Whenever a good monk, copying away on parchment, came across a Greek quotation or phrase in the middle of his Latin text, he calmly wrote in the classic expression

Table of concordances based on the gospels.

"graecum est, non legitur" or "this is Greek and cannot be read"!.

Saint Thomas of Aquinas clearly superseded Aristotle in the Christian world. But Homer, Herodotus, Aeschylus, Sophocles, Europides, Aristophanes, Pindar and Demosthenes were no better known in the Middle Ages than were the Alexandrians. The University of Paris had no faculty of Greek. One is inclined to forget that the Renaissance is said to have started with the fall of Constantinople to the Turks and the dispersal of the Greek element throughout the Europe of the 15th century. What is a humanist, when one really considers it, if not a man impregnated with Greek and Latin culture?

The literature which was brought back from Byzantium was to have a lasting and profound impact on the great movement for the restoration of the arts and literature in the 16th century.

The dual pagan and Christian nature of Byzantine was responsible for two notable features: its respect for the traditional forms of expression and purism of language, on the one hand, and a rigidity and hierarchy of the *genres* which deeply influenced literature deriving from Byzantium. Some writers tried to break out of the strict limits imposed by these principles; many of them were remarkably spontaneous, sensitive and imaginative, while their style drew heavily on the popular language.

From the 4th to the 6th century there was a transition from Hellenism to Byzantinism. This literary period is known, and rightly so, as the *pre-Byzantine* period. Besides Christian thinking, it involved some distinct pagan influences, a kind of swan-song of Ancient Greece. In the beginning, the major genres were sacred eloquence and theology, with famous Fathers of the Church such as St. John Chrysostom, or the members of the Cappadocian School. The main purpose of such a style was to convince and to convert.

In the 5th century, the trend was more towards explanation and the defense of dogma, in the face of numerous heresies. Great duels took place between ecclesiastics: Cyril, bishop of Alexandria debated with Nestorius, bishop of Antioch. Religious historiography was in the hands of scholars. Even secular literature was imbued with Christianity. However, the neo-Platonicians still wielded great influence over rhetoric, philosophy and poetry. Julian the Apostate had not been entirely forgotten.

Epic poety was imbued with paga-

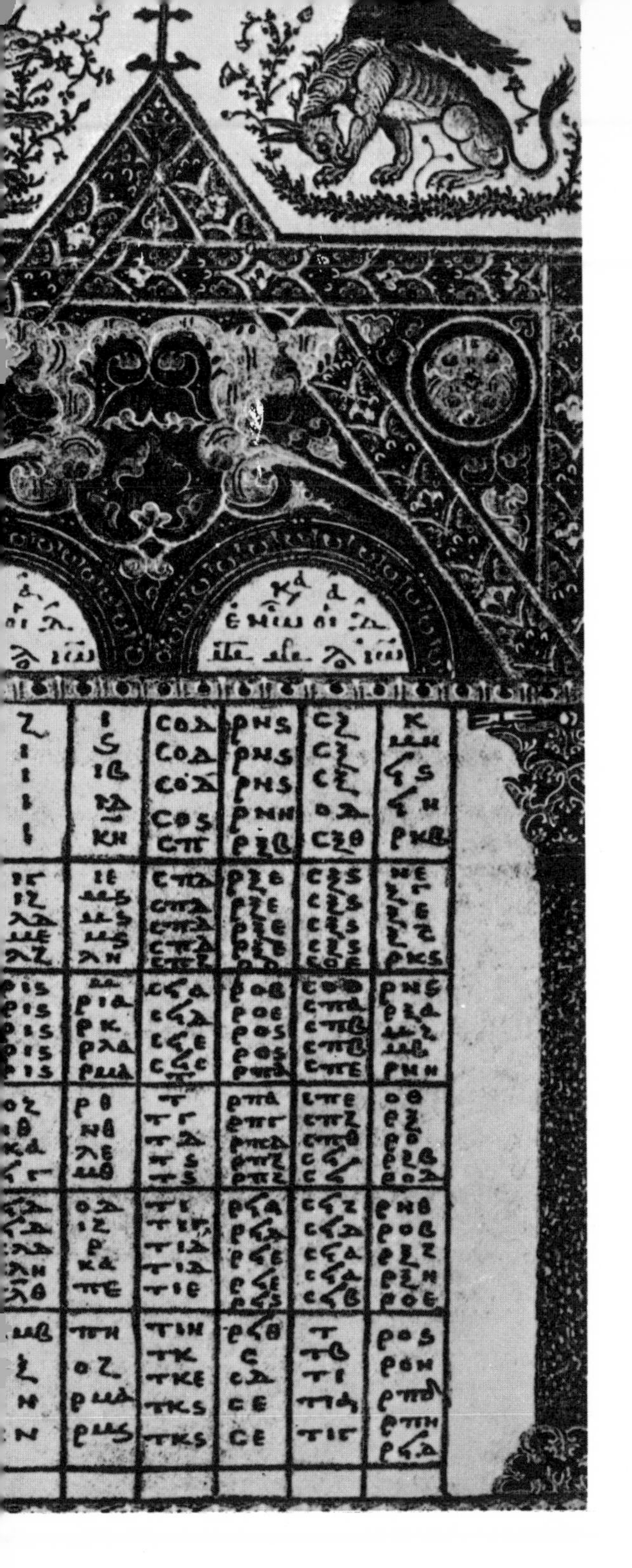

nism, as were the orphic poems which take us right back to the world of the Sibylline oracles. But the novel was the sphere in which the modern reader would be more likely to recognize works of true originality and value. Achilles Tatios wrote his great novel of love, the *Adventures of Leuci Leucippes and Clitophon,* the success was to continue until well into the Middle Ages. As for Longus, posterity was to attribute to him a masterpiece of grace and delicacy, *Daphnis and Cloe,* a pagan work which has lost none of its freshness.

This period lasted from the 6th to the 11th century, and is characterised by a distinctively Byzantine trait—religiosity.

The vast amount of religious literature which was produced was sometimes doctrinal and theological, as in the principal work of Leontius of Byzantium, *Libri tres adversus nestorianus et autychianos,* in which he attacked the theses of Nestorius and Eutyches. Or it could be didactic or ascetic, as in the case of Moshkos, whom one should not confuse with the charming Greek poet, the author of *Eros escaped.* The kind of thing which exercised the mind of the Byzantine Moshkos was in no way erotic. He lived among the anchorites before publishing his *Spiritual*

Meadow, a collection of highly edifying narratives. The work of Saint John Climatic, the *Holy Ladder*—the title of which accounts for his surname—is in the same vein. Religious literature could also be poetic, with the hymnographs or melods, of whom Rhômanos is the most famous because of his beauty of tone and the breadth of his inspiration. His canticle *Today the Virgin gives birth to Christ* was still one of the more popular Christmas carols until the 12th century.

History, even of the secular variety, was full of religious feeling. The famous historian Procopius lived under Justinian, starting as secretary to General Belisarius, and then becoming a court dignitary. His *Book of the Wars* is a fine combination of accuracy, a sense of detail, impartiality and, at the same time, interest on the part of the author. As for the *Anecdota,* their authenticity is open to question, but they are full of very colorful writing. Assuming that Procopius is in fact the author, this work shows that he was capable of great malice; Empress Theodora comes in for some rough treatment, in particular.

With each new heresy, religious literature rose to meet the challenge, attacking the Monotheists or the

Left: specimen of Byzantine handwriting.
Below: a portrait artist (miniature).

Iconoclasts, as the need arose. In the 8th century, Nicephorus and Theodora defended the advocates of religious imagery. John Damascenus and George Pisides were great theologians. Eventually this vein of inspiration ran dry, and the 9th century was to try another direction: the love of Antiquity emerged once more. This new humanism gave modern historians a work of capital importance, the *Myrioblion* or Library of Photius, an analytical collection of literary works, many of which have been lost. The 10th century saw a great flourishing of the Lives of the Saints, with Simon Metaphras and Kephalas. Emperor Constantine VII Porhyrogenete, was himself a historian of talent, though he tended to moralise rather than use strict scientific criteria. The most original art-form of the period was the one based on the epics and popular songs. A genuine epic cycle was built, around the adventures of Dhighenis Akritas, a a *chanson de geste* of courtly inspiration. Medieval literature can already be dimly discerned the lines of these works. In the theater the same thing was happening, with the creation of *Christ Suffering,* which was clearly a relative of the Western Miracle and Mystery Plays.

After the 11th century, the schism had caused a definitive breach between

Below, left: extract from a scientific manuscript. Right: two typical bas-reliefs (Athens).

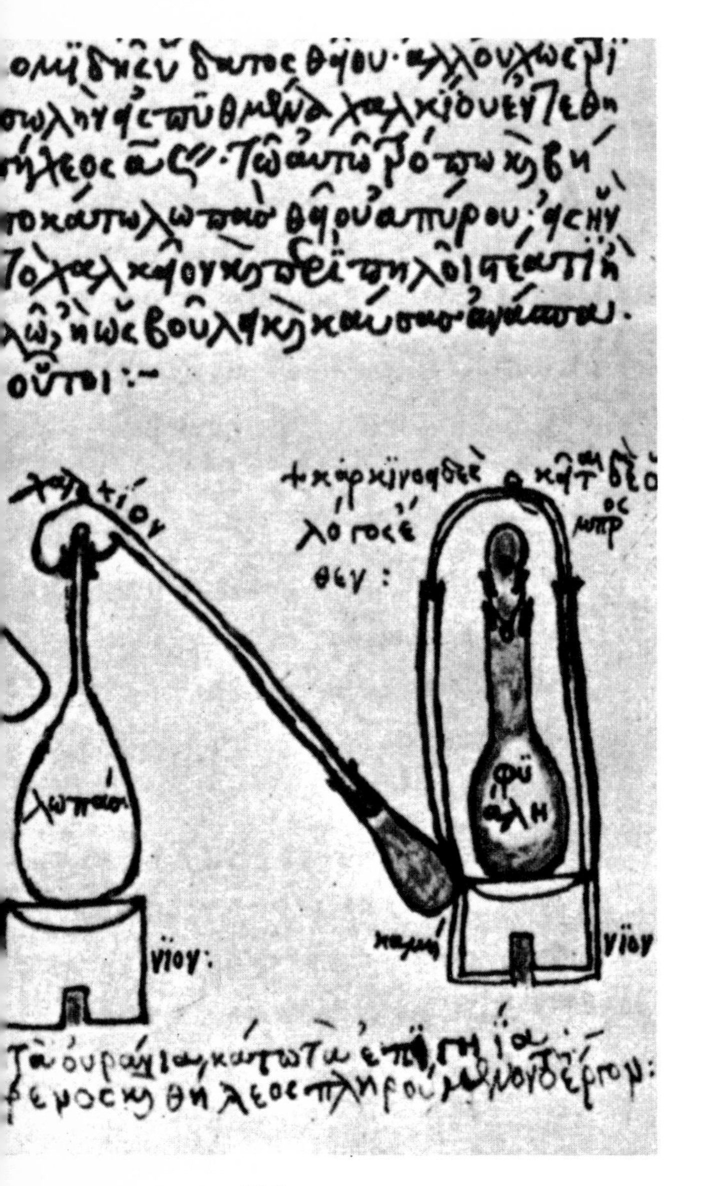

East and West. Humanism and independence of though were gaining ground, while theology was becoming philosophical with Psellos, who though Christian was a rationalist, mystical with Symeon, and moral with Cecaumenes. Imperial figures such as Anna Comnenus devoted their energies to subjects like history; attempts were even made at futurology. Prodomos, a legendary beggar poet, published burlesk and satirical poems.

Romanesque literature at that time produced works of the courtly genre, generally based on Antiquity, with a Christian flavor. The oriental tale was also popular. Then the influence of the Crusades made itself felt with the novels of chivalry in verse, such as *Belthandre and Chrysantza,* and *Callimachus and Chrysorrhoe.* Regions other than Constantinople were also the scene of flourishing literary activity about this time, for example Trebizonde and Mistra, which were to become the refuge of Hellenism when Byzantium fell to the Ottoman onslaught.

Under the Paleologues, literature recovers its brilliance one last time, with eminent names such as Pachymerus and Planudius. Philosophy lost its distinctively Byzantine traits and turned more towards the East and the West. As far as literary

thinking and philosophy were concerned, the 15th century was split right down the middle. One group was hostile to Latin thought, whereas another felt drawn by it. Emperor John IV Cantacuzenus was one the most famous historians of the period, together with Nicephorus Gregoras, Doukas and Phrantzes.

Byzantine art contains an intimate blend of Hellenistic art of the secular tradition of the countries of Asia Minor. The 3rd to the 5th centuries saw a decline of Greek art and a matching rise of oriental art, with a quest for a purely decorative style which meant the gradual abandonment of human representation. Its value lies particularly in the richness of textures, the delicate blending of colors and the hieratism of the composition itself. The ruins of Doura-Europos, in Syria, show a certain analogy with it, even before the Byzantine period properly so called. This Hellenistic city on Eastern soil was made up of a combination of three communities: Greek, Thracian and Persian, which is why its monuments contain disparate elements which later crop up in the monuments of Byzantium. At the time of the foundation of Byzantium this same semi-Greek oriental art was very much in fashion throughout the Empire. Under

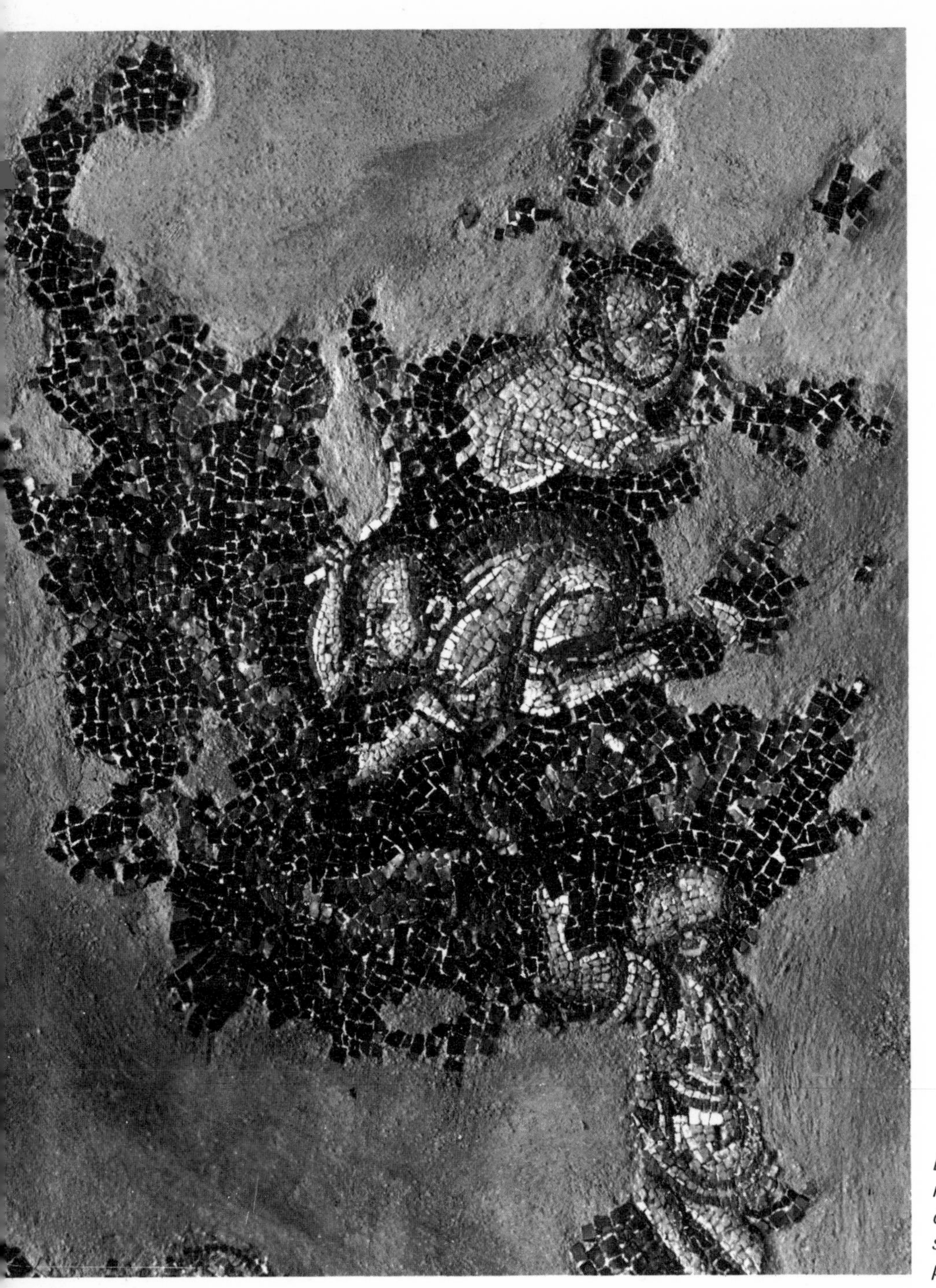

Left: birth of the mosaic. Right: detail of a mosaic (Hagia Sophia).

ΧΩ ΤΩ ΘΩ ΠΙϹΤΟϹ

Byzantine motifs.

Constantine, a great number of ancient monuments were raided, such was the Emperor's zeal for new building, and used to enrich the new structures. His successors also engaged in this sort of vandalism.

It was not until the 6th century that Constantinople saw the emergence of a original artistic school, or at least an independent one. Architecture then replaced the straight lines of the basilicas with the curves of the circular churches, and adopted the cupola placed on pendentives. Artists departed somewhat from strictly religious subjects, and started to decorate interiors with representations of secular historical scenes. The simplicity of the first period was now dropped in favor of sumptuous and resplendent mosaics, using a style much closer to reality, and much more figurative.

This art quickly spread beyond the borders of Byzantium. Its evolution can be classified in three periods: The Justinian, Macedonian and Palaeologi periods.

During the first period Byzantine art prospered as never before thanks to the huge programme of public works set in motion by Justinian. Between 527 and 565, it had certain distinctly oriental features. Those responsible for the conduct of the work were often themselves Asiatic in origin, such as Anthemios of Tralles and Isidore of Milet. The new techniques were also oriental; decorative sculpture replaced the use of modelling by means of a process which suggested the relief through the play of light. Lattice-

Mosaic from the floor of the transept of the Palatine Chapel, Palermo.

work sculpture also made its appearance. The master pieces of this period are the Church of the Holy Wisdom, Hagia Sophia, at Constantinople, Saints Serge and Baccnus, the Holy Apostles, also in Byzantium, Saint Vital and Saint Appolinarius at Ravenna. The same tendencies occurred in the minor arts, such as illuminated manuscripts and miniatures.

The next period left us few works, most of them having been destroyed. During the 7th and 8th centuries, while the Empire was busy fending off Arab and Slav raids, Byzantine art fell into a decline. Contrary to what one might expect, Iconoclasm was not hostile to art. Far from it, during this struggle, religious art became stronger. Emperors tended to favor a style which blended the ancient and the Arab styles. Armenian and Georgian influences also were apparent. The church in those days was built in the form of a Greek cross inserted in a square. Brick was used increasingly, and, with the new ceramics and other new materials, a brilliant array of colors could be used. The walls were now no longer smooth–there were niches in various positions, to break up the larger shape. Arcades were also common, as were windows. The most remarkable of these new monuments, built between 867 and 1057, are the New Church of Basil I, at Constantinople, the Hagia Sophia at Ohrid, in Greece, and the Smaller Metropolis, in Athens.

As it developed, the monastic influence restored the former preponderant role of the Christian traditions, as can be seen from the miniatures from this period which were painted on manuscripts (Gregory of Nazianzius, 9th century; Psalter of the 10th century, Bibliothèque Nationale, Paris; Menelogue of Basil II, Vatican). As for ornamental work in bronze or ivory, and the enamels and fine fabrics, they were as brilliant and lavish as ever.

Despite the Latin conquest on 1204, which seemed to have sounded the deathknell of the Byzantine Empire, the traditional civilisation survived and even consolidated its position. Artistic centers were being formed all the time. Besides Constantinople and Thessalonika, new poles of attraction were being formed, such as Trebizond and Mistra. The ancient cupola style re-appeared at Trebizond with Saint Eugene and Chrysocephalos. At Mistra, on the other hand, there was a mixture of styles ranging from the Latin-cross type of architecture, for example at Evanghelistria, to the Greek cross of

MELCHISEDEC

The very pinnacle of Byzantine art, Ravenna.

the Saints Theodore at Broutochion. Painting flourished as never before. This is the moment when the great resurrection of the art of Antiquity began—the same trend which later reconquered Italy and the whole of the Christian West, burgeoning into the colossal revolutionary movement known as the Renaissance. It all began at Constantinople. Yet again, Greek civilisation gave its light to the Western world.

Ever since the foundation of Byzantium, music had been one of the most important arts. Of course, we are talking about sacred music. The liturgical order had been fixed in the 4th century by Basil the Great and John Chrysostom. Then, hymnography developed with the melod poets, among them Gregory of Nazianzius, the patriarchs Proclus and Anatolius, Romanus the Melod, Andrew of Crete, John of Damascus and many others. Religious hymns were simply sung by human voices. In the 9th century a great poetess named Kassia emerged; thereafter, melody began to decline. The ancient melodies were now transformed, "embellished" and adorned with flourishes which were not always in the best taste.

A new style, the melismatic style, emerged in the 14th century, with John Cucuzeles who reformed musical

The two wides of a medal dedicated to John VIII Paleologus, emperor of Constantinople.

notation; indeed, since that time, his name has been given to the reformed notation. Much later, it was to be further reformed by Christian of Madyte, under the influence of a reformist trend in the 19th century, due to the new influence of Western music in the Christian East.

Just when the Christian East was collapsing under the onslaught of the Muslims, who had seized Constantinople in the name of the Holy War, literature and art both took refuge in Western Europe where they survived, uncomfortably at first and later flourished in a great upsurge of new vitality. Their influence was to be a decisive factor in the further progress of civilisation.

As we have seen, at the origin of the Renaissance in the 16th century, Greek and Byzantine thought were to give birth, as it were, to the modern world.

Bas-relief with the head of a Turk.

11/The fall of a civilization

In the medieval world two civilisations stood confronting one another: that of the Gospel and that of the Koran. As if by some kind of tacit understanding, you might almost say a Yalta before the event, there was a *de facto* agreement. The trouble with Byzantium was that it was situated right at the hinge between these two worlds: that was the cause of its final misfortunes.

While Christian society governed the whole of Europe, except for Muslim-occupied Spain, the Greek world of Byzantium looked more and more like an island which had not yet been submerged by the flood tide of invasions. It was aging and visibly sagging. Ever since Justinian, its political life had been going round in circles, with a succession of emperors grasping and then losing power through crime and palace intrigues. There was a great deal of gouging out of eyes, castration and killing as soon as the new emperor reached his goal, only to suffer the same fate a short while later. Theological quarrels often turned into rioting. Byzantium muddled through, fending off the attacks of the masters of Asia one day, and of the Northern barbarians the next. The schism between the two Churches, which had begun with the Iconoclasts, was still alive. Now it had become permanent, with the inclusion of the world *filioque* by the Latin Church in the Nicene Creed, and as a result of certain differences of rite: the use of leavened instead of unleavened bread, marriage for priests, baptism by immersion, the use of the vernacular in ceremonies, fasting on Saturday. Behind all these differences, of course, lay the great rivalry between the two Churches, of Rome and Constantinople.

Left on its own, separated from the Christian West, the Byzantine Empire long found it could manage with its resources and its emperors to keep its frontiers intact, and even to get the upper hand over its enemies from time to time. Late in the 9th century, the Turkish Empire was weakened: on the death of Malek-Shah, in the words of a Persian poet, "a great host of princes rose up at his feet". In other words, the Ottoman Empire was breaking up, being replaced by large numbers of individual sultanates. Even so, at the beginning of the First Crusade, the whole of Asia Minor was in Turkish hands.

The Fourth Crusade was the one which was to shake Byzantium to the foundations. It was intended to strike as much at the Greeks, who had massacred so many Latins, as the Turks. 4,500 knights, under the

Two representations of a naval battle: the clash of two enemy vessels.

orders of Thibaut de Champagne, were at Venice loading the vessels made available to the army by the Doge, when the son of former Basileus Isaac II, Alexius, came and asked for aid and protection against his uncle Alexius III, who had usurped his throne. His uncle had had his eyes gouged out... as was the custom in such cases. He promised the knights ten thousand troops and assured the Pope that the Eastern Church would submit to Rome if Isaac the Blind was put back on the throne. The crusaders' fleet was shortly about to land at Chalcedon, which was separated from Constantinople by a canal only five miles long. The crusaders attacked furiously. The usurper-Basileus, Alexius III, took fright and ran away. Isaac II was released from the prison where he had been vegetating and his wife, who had been shut up in a cloister, was reunited with him. The young Alexius was crowned and made a triumphant entry into the capital, throwing himself into his father's arms.

The aftermath was not so favorable. The crusaders insisted on the fulfilment of the treaty signed in Venice, demanding payment to them of two hundred thousand pounds of gold, which was a lot of gold for a people already in dire straits. Also, the Patriarch, in the church of Hagia Sophia, had to make his submission to the Pope and recognize him as supreme head of the Christian Church. Alexius IV was beginning to find his Latin allies a distinct nuisance, and the Byzantine people viewed them with horror. One day, some Frenchmen were stabbed to death by a small band commanded by John Ducas, otherwise known as Murzuphle, and the Greeks tried to burn the Latin fleet. Alexius nevertheless agreed to pay the tribute, but, when Constantinople heard of it there was a massive popular uprising: the mob wanted a new emperor. For a while, the outcome was uncertain; eventually Murzuphle was crowned, but not before he had personally strangled Alexius IV. The father of Alexius, Isaac the Blind, died suddenly of shock, and the new Basileus acceded to the throne. One of his first acts was the laying of a trap for the crusaders, by inviting them to a conference, having first posted soldiers on the premises in order to have them all murdered. The Latins owed their lives to the Doge, Dandelo, who, being a wily old fox himself, suspected something was wrong. But they were furious and attacked the Greek troops, who then fell back towards Constantinople. Attempts at conciliation failed and the crusaders then stormed the city. Murzuphle,

ναυμαχία
τὸν τῶν ἐναντίων στόλον

whose reign had lasted one fleeting moment, fled for his life, and was replaced on the battlefield, in the midst of the action, by Theodore Lascaris. The new emperor, in a state of suppressed rage, had to abandon his capital, his sole consolation being the hope that one day he might return to it in triumph.

The crusaders, however, offered the throne to the Doge of Venice, Dandelo. A citizen of Venice opposed this decision, saying: "If our Doge is on the throne of Byzantium our freedom will be at an end and the Republic will be merely a province of the Empire." Dandelo wisely echoed these sentiments, and Baudouin, Count of Flanders, was elected in his place. Hoisted high on a shield, he was carried into Hagia Sophia, where a solemn coronation took place.

The crusaders promptly set about dismembering the Empire; the feudal system replaced the ancient constitutions, each baron becoming the lord of one or more cities. The Pope was sent a wealth of gifts and large numbers of relics were sent to Philippe-Auguste. The Venetian Thomas Morosini was elected Patriarch. The authority of the Holy See was to be recognized everywhere, except in the cities of Asia which espoused the cause of Lascaris.

Constantine's empire thus collapsed, in 1204. Theirs is an example to be carefully pondered by those people who called in foreign support and arms to solve their internal discord.

Then came the rush for the spoils.

The capture of Constantinople by the crusaders was followed by the construction on the ruins of the Byzantine Empire of the Latin Empire of Constantinople, and a whole series of Frankish principalities in the feudal style. All that remained of the Greek Empire was the Despotate of Epirus, in the hands of the Comneni, Trebizond and the Empire of Nicaea. This latter had been founded by Theodore Lascaris (1204-1261) when he had been forced, by the crusaders' onslaught, to flee his capital. This Empire of Nicaea was to be the custodian of Hellenism in the East throughout the Frankish occupation. It was from there that the troops of Michael Palaeologus set out on the way to Constantinople, which they took on July 25 1261, as Emperor Baudouin II and the Latin Patriarch hastily abandoned the city and fled.

The Franks had left behind them a totally exhausted Empire. The palaces and mansions of Constantinople fell into decay, while the Eastern trade was now entirely in the hands of Venice and Genoa. Its territory had now

shrivelled up, until it consisted solely of Nicaea, in Asia, and Thrace and parts of Macedonia, in Europe. It was a monster with an outsize head, Constantinople, and virtually nothing else. This hydrocephalous empire was, for more than two centuries, to be the "sick man" just like the Ottoman Empire in the 19th century.

All that is known about the history of this final period of Byzantine history is that, after some success achieved by Michael Palaeologus, his successors tried to put off the evil day as long as possible. Faced with fantastic financial difficulties, their main problem was tax-collection: everything that could be taxed was taxed, and everything that could be sold was sold. When it came to the marriage of John V, not a single piece of gold or silver plate could be found anywhere in the palace. The precious stones in the jewelry had long ago been replaced by cheap imitations. The military settlers, groaning under an incredible tax burden, simply abandoned their land, thus leaving the frontiers wide open to enemy forces. The fleet had been badly neglected and it now lay rotting in harbor, while the mercenaries, who were being paid only spasmodically, either deserted or revolted.

Byzantium was dying a slow death. Yet, even during its final agony, religious squabbles continued. The Zealots—or Arsenites, after the Patriarch, Arsenius—counted on the monks and the people to resist the emperor's policies. They were in favor of strict orthodoxy and totally opposed to any concessions to Rome. At the same time, Gregory Palamas, a monk from Mount Athos Archbishop of Thessalonika, had been preaching a doctrine called *hesychasm* (Greek for "tranquillity") which became immensely popular. During the reign of the Palaeologus emperors a number of contemplative monks from Mount Athos were to become Patriarchs. Just when stern action and military prowess was most needed, all that was being proposed was the eucharistic host and meditation. This was the permanent flaw of Byzantium. Unlike most of the princes of Europe, who were careful to prevent the Church from encroaching on their powers, most of the Byzantine Emperors allowed themselves to be swamped by the Church. For the Capetians, for example, the Church was a means of consolidating the State, whereas for the Basileus, it was an end... his own end, as it happened.

From the 13th century onwards the Eastern world had witnessed the rise of Turkish power. Osman—or

Othman—had been the founder of the dynasty of the Osmanlis—or Ottomans; he made a small tribe which had been driven westwards by the Mongols into a powerful and warlike State, most of whose military energies had been directed, at an early date, against Byzantium. In the middle of the 14th century, the Turks were masters of virtually all of Asia Minor. John V Cantacuzenus used them to accede to the throne and even married his daughter to Sultan Orkhan. He authorised them to settle at a fortified point on the European shore of the Straits. But this did not assuage this ambitions of the Ottomans, who soon conquered all of Thrace, Philippopoli and Andrinople, where Sultan Murad I made his capital. The hapless John V was wasting his time going to Rome seeking help... to crown his misfortunes, he was imprisoned on his return—for debts he had contracted in Venice! His son Manuel had to pay to obtain the release of his father.

In 1399 Manuel II went to the European courts to beg for help. He made a splendid entry into Paris where Charles VI had plenty of the other worries at the time, as he had the English on his territory. From London Manuel came away full of promises, but little else.

In 1402 the crushing defeat suffered by the Turks at the hands of Tamerlan's Mongol hordes gave the Empire some twenty years' breathing space. However, as soon as 1430 the Ottomans seized Thessalonika. Through the decree of Union signed by John VIII and Pope Eugene IV, the Holy See did try to raise a small army of Hungarians, Poles and Romanians which, led by Vladislav, King of Hungary, tried to relieve the hard-pressed Eastern Christians, but it was cut to ribbons at Varna in 1444.

From then on the West took no further interest in the fate of the Eastern Empire. In 1451 Mohammed II became sultan and, after cutting communications between Byzantium and the Black Sea, he laid siege to Constantinople in April 1453.

Emperor Constantine XII was in charge of the defense of the city. It is curious that the last Eastern emperor bore the same name as the founder of the capital, just as the last emperor of Rome was called Romulus, like the one who had traced out the limits of the future city with the blade of his plow. However, there was a difference between the two: Romulus was a figure of derision, nicknamed *Augustulus* by the Romans, whereas Constantine XII fought to the very end. Byzantium, under siege, saw its walls crumbing under the battering of powerful artillery. On May 28 it was discovered, through prisoners, that the Turks were going to make the final assault at dawn the next day. Processions were then held that same evening and the last Christian services in history were held in the basilica of Hagia Sophia.

Next day, at the head of the few able-bodied Christian soldiers left–most of them Genovese mercenaries–Constantine XII, the last Emperor of the East, fell in action while defending Christian civilisation and the Western World, neither of which had realized that Byzantium was their last position in Asia Minor. Before long, Europe would be fighting back the Turkish invaders on its own soil.

Mohammed II rode into Hagia Sophia and his janissaries proceeded to massacre the crowd of women and children who had taken refuge there. Untold atrocities were committed there. That same day, the cross was taken down from the pinnacle of the sacred edifice, to be replaced by the crescent.

For three days and nights plunder and killings went on. "The Turks have been this way, all is ruin and grief".

Byzantium is now dead for ever. Its only chance of survival would have been an agreement between Greeks and Latins; this was clear at least to its last sovereigns, the Palaeologi. Yet they had to contend with the ambitions of the Pope and also with the lack of understanding shown by the West and the sectarian sentiments of the Byzantines. Petrarch went so far as to say: "The Turks are our enemies, but the schismatic Greeks are worse than enemies." About the same time an eminent magistrate from Constantinople exclaimed: "I would sooner see the Turkish turban in power in Constantinople than the Latin mitre!" The worst enemy is often our own brother! Empires fall under external pressures when they are divided and rotten within. This is a law of history which everbody knows, but which no-one thinks about at the right moment.

The Greeks who had been expelled from Byzantium were to carry with them to the West, which had abandoned them, their culture and also their science. They were to be one of the most vital motive forces behind the colossal revolution of men's thinking which we call the Renaissance.

While the green banners of the Prophet were reflected in the waters of the Sea of Marmara, the Greek cross carried the age-old heritage of Greco-Roman civilisation to the banks of the Seine, the Tiber and the Rhine.